Winning Letters
That **Overcome Barriers**
to **Employment**

Daniel Porot and *Frances Bolles Haynes*

IMPACT PUBLICATIONS
Manassas Park, VA

Winning Letters That Overcome Barriers to Employment

ISBN: 1-57023-254-7

Library of Congress: 2006922504

Publisher: For information on Impact Publications, including current and forthcoming publications, authors, press kits, online bookstore, and submission requirements, visit our website: www.impactpublications.com.

Sales/Distribution: All bookstore sales are handled through Impact's trade distributor: National Book Network, 15200 NBN Way, Blue Ridge Summit, PA 17214, Tel. 1-800-462-6420. All other sales and distribution inquiries should be directed to the publisher: Sales Department, IMPACT PUBLICATIONS, 9104 Manassas Drive, Suite N, Manassas Park, VA 20111-5211, Tel. 703-361-7300, Fax 703-335-9486, or email: query@impactpublications.com.

The Authors: Daniel Porot, an internationally recognized career expert who resides in Switzerland, is the author of numerous career books. Frances Bolles Haynes has been active in the career development field for over 20 years. They regularly offer career-training workshops and seminars. This is the third book they have collaborated on.

Table of Contents

Foreword.. v

Introduction 1

Section 1: Successful Job Hunting

1 The Real Barriers to Employment 7

2 Letters and the Job Hunting Process...................... 11

3 The Open Market 18

4 Using the Want Ads 24

5 The Hidden Job Market 27

6 Increasing the Odds... 38

7 Sensitive Issues 49

8 The Purpose of a Cover Letter 56

Section 2: Building Your Letter Step By Step

9 Step 1: The Sender's Information 69

10 Step 2: The Date 74

11 Step 3: The Recipient 78

12 Step 4: The Reference Line 85

13 Step 5: The Salutation 91

14 Step 6: The Opening Paragraph 95

15 Step 7: The Body of the Letter 103

16 Step 8: A "Call to Action" Paragraph 119

17 Step 9: The Complimentary Closing..126

18 Step 10: The Signature 130

19 Step 11: Enclosures 135

20 Step 12: The Postscript 140

Section 3: The Nuts and Bolts

21 Design and Layout 145

22 Paper and Envelope..150

23 Delivery 154

24 Writing Style 158

Appendix A: Writing Your Achievement Paragraphs 167

Appendix B: Letter Examples 181

Appendix C: Unsolicited Letter Quiz Answers and Rationale 205

Index...212

Career Resources..215

Foreword

We would like to dedicate this book to the thousands of job seekers and employers who have told us over these past 30+ years what works well and what doesn't work so well, as they have navigated the job hunting waters and . . . found jobs. We owe a debt of gratitude to every person who has bravely and unflinchingly tried a new technique or different method of job hunting, flying valiantly in the face of convention and then been willing to share their insights and success stories with us.

We have made every effort to provide accurate and useful information that is results-oriented and able to be put into operation immediately. In this ever changing world, both the economic and job hunting landscapes alter, transform, and adjust to new forces all the time (sometimes seemingly every day). For this reason, the information we provide herein may not always be the most up-to-date information possible, particularly as it relates to the Internet and websites, which come and go as the wind shifts. We provide it for reference purposes only, believing it to be accurate at the time of our writing.

And finally, a note about our language: Most readers find it burdensome and difficult to read text when writers use the "he/she" pronoun after a singular subject. We find this a rather inelegant and clumsy way to write, so, based on the recommendations of readers, we have chosen to use the plural pronouns "they," "their," and "them," when referring to an often singular subject. We are opting for agreement in gender over agreement in number, and hope not to offend anyone.

Introduction

This book is about how to write a letter to an employer. Doesn't sound too glamorous or exciting, we know! But when it's done right it can make a huge difference in how a job hunter is perceived by an employer and ultimately in the very success of the job hunting effort.

In this book you will:

1. Learn how to use a fail-safe 12-step approach that covers everything about writing effective letters that observe proper rules and etiquette and use persuasive language.

2. Examine every part of a letter, starting with the sender's name and address and moving through to the postscript.

3. Discover how you can easily write a cover letter with confidence, originality, and style.

4. Increase your chances for job search success by crafting letters that will stand out and make an employer want to learn more about you.

We wrote this book to teach you, the job hunter, how to present yourself to an employer for your **first contact** with them, whether invited in with an ad or job posting, or approaching an employer on your own initiative, usually called an "unsolicited approach." If you do this well, you will master the tools you need to gain the upper hand in your job hunting efforts. By concentrating on this one specific area, you increase your chances to be invited for an interview.

So, what might seem like a small step turns out to be one of the most important steps in the job search process. When you've mastered this first approach by producing outstanding letters, your efforts will pay off and you will have a better chance to get the result you want. You could be a perfect candidate for a job, but if your first introduction to a prospective employer isn't done right, it probably won't matter. You will miss your chance.

You may have heard that expression, *"You are what you eat."* Only for our purposes here, it's, *"You are what you write."* If you underestimate the importance of this one first step and fail to make a good impression on employers, you will spend more time, energy, and money than you want, and you'll miss job opportunities that might have been a good match for you. Don't let that happen because you didn't know how to do it right or you didn't care enough to give it your best shot.

This book deals mostly with what has come to be known as the **"Cover Letter"** (also called Letter of Introduction, Letter of Application, T-Letter, Broadcast Letter, Letter of Inquiry, or Referral Letter). It is that first letter sent to a prospective employer to introduce yourself. It might be in response to an advertisement placed by an employer (called the Open Market) or might be an "unsolicited" letter, where you take the initiative to contact an employer without waiting for an ad to appear (called the Hidden Market).

You might wonder, *"What's the big deal? It's only a letter after all,"* but if it's the first (and sometimes only) contact with someone you want something from, namely a meeting – and perhaps then a job, you need to get it right. It's the paper ambassador you send to represent who you are – so make it the best you can. It's a mistake to give your letters short shrift, assuming your resume can stand alone and impress an employer so much they will call you in for an interview. They might, but you increase your chances for that outcome by including a good cover letter that tells the employer something more. If you don't stand out from others, your resume may not even get a glance.

We doubt you would go to meet someone whom you wanted to impress without preparing and trying to put your best foot forward. The same holds true here. Make your letters count!

The advice we offer has been culled from working with over 70,000 job hunters during the last 30+ years, who have told us, time and again, what strategy, technique, or style has worked most effectively. There is no such thing as perfection. If you strive for that, you will make yourself and those around you crazy! Instead, strive to do the best you can do, be the best you can be, and change your plan when it isn't working. That's all you can do.

All advice and recommendations in this book are "situational." What you do will depend on the situation you are in. We don't intend to make you believe there are absolute rules which, if broken, will somehow turn you into a frog! Sometimes one strategy or technique will work, sometimes another. Not every technique will fit your personality or style. You might read a suggestion and think to yourself, *"I could never do that in a million years!"* That's okay. You're free to accept or reject our ideas as too risky or maybe even ludicrous, or maybe you'll think, *"That'll take way too much time!"* When you say or think any of those things, just ask yourself these questions:

1. *Is what I am currently doing (or not doing) working for me?*
2. *Am I any closer to finding that job I want?*
3. *How am I spending my time?*
4. *Have I done my homework?* (Yes, there's homework even when you aren't in school!)
5. *Are the strategies and techniques I've been using moving me any closer to finding the job I want?*
6. *What have I got to lose if I try something new or different?*

If you like the answers you come up with when you ask yourself these questions, then keep on doing what you're doing. If you don't like them, consider trying something new. Make a change. Take the risk. Open your mind.

Finally, we know that not all of us have stellar backgrounds – never a career misstep – never a problem with job performance – never a problem with personal issues – never a problem with defining characteristics (like gender, age, nationality) – never a problem with supervisors and bosses, etc. With the exception of a handful of people (there are some), all of us have sensitive issues we face when hunting for a job. This book seeks to deal with those issues and help you overcome them in honest, responsible ways. There is always more than one way to say anything, and presenting yourself in the best light is possible, while maintaining truth and integrity. It just takes understanding why, when, and how you should mention sensitive areas.

This book is divided into three main sections.

1. **Section One** is a general overview of job hunting, as it's currently done, and how to increase your chance for success. Section One explains both the Open and Hidden Markets, the reason for ads, and how to overcome sensitive issues. Finally, it describes why cover letters are important.

2. **Section Two** details in a step-by-step process each part of a cover letter and how to easily construct a letter. Every chapter takes on one part of the letter and outlines the location in the letter, reason, purpose, difficulty, importance, specifics, do's and don'ts, and examples, both good and bad, for that element of the letter. Chapter 15 includes 36 sample achievement statements/paragraphs that demonstrate how achievements might be written up. These are included for illustrative purposes to show how the use of quantifiable facts and figures adds strength to your letter.

3. **Section Three** covers the "nuts and bolts" about these letters, and answers the frequently asked questions about design, layout, length, ink color, paper and envelope, delivery, and writing styles and tips.

The book also includes three appendices:

1. **Appendix A** contains forms and exercises to help you better write the body of your letter. You will find exercises that are designed to aid in writing "achievement" statements/paragraphs that can be used in your letters to help employers better understand what you have done in the past and how it can relate to the job(s) you are interested in pursuing. A list of "action verbs" is provided to help you get started.

2. **Appendix B** contains sample cover letters demonstrating different styles that might be used for cover letters. Each letter contains comments that outline what the author of the letter was accomplishing.

3. **Appendix C** contains the rationale for the answers to the Quiz on the Unsolicited Approach at the beginning of Chapter 5.

1 Section One
Successful Job Hunting

Chapter 1

The Real Barriers to Employment

I t's a mistake to think that the biggest barriers we face when looking for a job have to do with being too old or too young, male or female, overqualified or underqualified, too general or too specific in our skills and knowledge, having a criminal record, being too thin or too heavy, hearing impaired or wheelchair bound, black, white, red, or purple. While those issues can have an impact on you, they are not ultimately what stands between you and the job you want. What stands between that job and you is something you can control. Thankfully!

> It turns out the biggest barriers to employment relate to our knowledge about how to best approach employers.

The Biggest Barriers

It turns out the biggest barriers most people face when looking for a job are not knowing two important things: 1) whom to approach when we job hunt, and 2) how to approach those employers correctly once we find them. We don't do it right and because we do it wrong, we lose out. We don't get our letter or resume read when we send it to the wrong person. We don't get invited for an interview when our letter fails to impress. We don't get the job we want. We don't reach our goal. We don't make the connection that could have shown someone, "Yes, I can do this job!"

We lose out because we:

- Send our applications, letters, and resumes to the wrong people.
- Fail to understand the needs of employers (or our own needs).

- Undervalue or don't value our achievements and qualifications.
- Avoid trying new and different job-hunting approaches – moving "outside the box" with our strategies.
- Don't research the recipient, field, company, and/or job content of our letters and resumes.
- Act like a "Job-Beggar" and not a "Resource Person."
- Make spelling or grammatical mistakes.
- Send the same letter or resume to every employer.
- Use the ME-ME-ME approach, instead of the YOU-ME-WE approach.
- Limit ourselves before we even get started and fail to pursue our dreams.

Making Good Choices

The good news is that we can overcome these barriers and even eliminate them! Since such barriers are not placed on us from outside, as is the case with prejudice and bias from others, we can control how we deal with them. We can make the **choice** to learn what works and implement it. We can move the odds in our favor for positive outcomes.

You have the power within you to make key choices by:

- Educating yourself.
- Researching recipients, fields, companies, and job content.
- Risking new behaviors, even when they run counter to what you've been taught before.
- Conducting self-assessment exercises.
- Targeting your job search.
- Listening to the feedback of others.
- Placing the employer first.
- Knowing when to address a sensitive issue.
- Caring enough to send documents without mistakes.
- Tailoring your approach to each individual company or person contacted.
- Valuing effectiveness over efficiency.

Taking control and understanding that knowing who to approach and how to approach (those employers once you've found them) makes all the difference in our success, and barriers crumble and disappear when we do it right.

How Job Hunting Should Go

If we outlined the way most people would like job hunting to work, it would go like this:

1. I want a job.
2. I know what I want to do.
3. I know where I want to do it.
4. When I'm ready, the job I want to do, in the place I want to do it, will be ready and waiting for me.
5. I'll apply for the job.
6. I'll get the job.
7. I'll like my salary.
8. I'll celebrate!

Wouldn't that be lovely?

Maybe you know someone who has had this experience of job hunting; maybe it's even you! All the pieces miraculously fall into place at the right time, and job hunting is a snap. No muss, no fuss. Destiny has stepped in and made sure you were matched with your dream job.

It could go like that . . . every once in a while.

Successful Job Hunters

Even for most who easily find their way through the maze of job hunting, however, destiny doesn't play nearly as a big a role as hard work, preparation, planning, following up, and being willing to try new strategies when the old ones don't work. Successful job hunters look for ways around *"there is only one way to find a job,"* and they risk rejection from time to time, knowing they will survive it. They become proactive, instead of reactive. They try writing, calling, visiting, and, now, surfing the Web to find the information they need. They understand that a "no" may come before a "yes" (*no, no ...yes!!*), and they don't let the "no" diminish their efforts. They ask questions, they seek answers, and they feel reassured deep down that, in the final analysis, what they have to offer is useful, needed, and wanted by employers. They put their best foot forward and take the time to do it right with whatever strategy they use. They understand what worked last time might not work this time, so they leave their options open and try new strategies – when those old ones don't work.

> Even when you are really good at what you do, you may not be good at getting the job you want.

This isn't to say that job hunting isn't a complex and arbitrary process, even for those good at the mechanics of it. **Even when you are really good at what you do, you may not be good at getting the job you want.** Job hunting takes time, persistence, energy, and an ability to keep your spirits up in the face of rejection. It takes knowing, either by your own experience or the wisdom of others, what works best and what doesn't work so well, as you maneuver your way through what is commonly called the "job hunting" process.

Chapter 2

Letters and the Job Hunting Process

When we hear the term "job hunting," different images, thoughts and feelings surface in us, depending on our experience. For some, job hunting is no big deal. They are good at it and they do it with ease, willing to embrace the challenge of the process with gusto. They are successful at it and often receive more than one job offer. They experiment with different strategies and don't put all their eggs in one basket – in other words, they don't just blindly send out resumes to Internet sites.

For other people, job hunting ranks right up there with getting major dental work done without anesthetic, or running a marathon with little or no training. They dread it and feel immobilized and paralyzed by it. They approach it with fear and pessimism. They are unsure what strategy to use and generally stick to only one approach – like just blindly sending out resumes to Internet sites.

> Job hunting is part science, part art, and part luck. Luck, in most cases, being 90% preparation!

Job Search Science, Art, and Luck

What you surely know, if you've done it even once, is that job hunting isn't a science. There is no way to tell you that in 100% of the cases this strategy or this technique will work. There are just too many variables to be able to say, with certainty, that there is only one way to do it. Every job hunter is different, every employer is different, every job is different, and timing can never be the same twice.

11

It would be lovely if job hunting were a science that we knew would involve ever constant, never changing facts and we could count on the same rules and practices working each and every time to get a positive outcome. It will never be like that! It's pretty difficult to have hard and fast rules when human beings get involved in the process. It's much more realistic to look at job hunting as part science, part art, and part luck. Luck, in most cases, being 90% preparation!

What we can tell you with some certainty after studying this field for many years is, **we know it works better when you**:

- have identified WHAT you want to do, WHERE you want to do it, and HOW to go about job hunting strategically.
- are specific and targeted in your approach.
- can talk to actual people, rather than sending some kind of paper messenger to deliver your information.
- don't lie about who you are and what you have done and can do.
- are not alone and without resources.
- seek to find your dream job.

Employers Focus on Managing Numbers

For the employer, the job hunting process is about expediency. It has become a numbers game, and it's understandable why a company that receives 20,000 unsolicited resumes a month might like some easy way to whittle down this number into something manageable. So, the format of a one (or two at most) page document outlining some high points of a person's experience has become the standard way to categorize, reduce the number of potential applicants and eliminate those that don't interest them. The primary focus is to narrow down these numbers (of candidates) into a small enough group from which a decision about whom to interview or hire becomes realistic. Even smaller companies with fewer numbers of applicants want some kind of effective system to deal with hiring. Hence, the resume. For those untrained in the art of interviewing, having a resume to follow as a guide makes it easier. No need to stray outside the facts listed on the paper when asking questions.

Job Hunters Focus on Effectiveness

For the job hunter, the job hunting process is about making a good impression. Job hunters are interested in getting their information out in a way that will impress and, in the best of cases, dazzle a potential employer into wanting to hire them. A one- or two-page document doesn't allow for that in most cases, especially when the document's primary focus is on the past and not the future.

We know the numbers game is not in the best interest of the job hunter because it doesn't take into account a person's uniqueness or allow for detailed demonstration of a person's potential.

Perception and Reality

Unfortunately for most job hunters, the resume has evolved as the primary tool of introduction. Resumes and CVs (Curriculum Vitae) are widely preferred by many employers because they are expedient. They save time and money – a recruiter or interviewer can look through hundreds of letters and resumes in a day, on average taking from 10 seconds to one minute per document, and never once have to interact with another person.

Consider these two common "rules" about resumes: **perception vs. reality.**

> **RULE #1:** *It is considered practically impossible to get a job offer without handing over a resume.*

This is the perception.

> **RULE #2:** *The later you hand over your resume (or skip it altogether), the better your chance to get the job and not be screened out too early.*

This is the reality.

How to marry Rule #1 with Rule #2 is the trick!

What the Job Hunter Can Do

Because employers **love** resumes for their expediency, even knowing how inadequate they are to tell the whole story, they often ask for them when screening candidates for interviews. It appears to many job hunters that they "must" therefore use their resume when they look for a job.

However, this approach doesn't work well for most of us. Job hunters do have power in this process, since each side needs the other for the match. Job hunters also have resourcefulness, creativity, and the ability to bend the rules to their advantage by:

- Contacting line managers directly.
- Sending a well-crafted cover letter without a resume (no, that's not heresy!).
- Using contacts to gain direct access to someone who might be interested in them.

- Using portfolios, which could include certificates, photos, press clippings, etc., instead of resumes to show what they have done and can do.

When You Do Use a Resume

Since it is not likely that resumes and CVs in their current form will go away anytime soon, if you do choose to use one, consider this advice:

1. Shorter is better than longer.
2. Specific is better than general.
3. Customized is better than standard.
4. Quantified and illustrated is better than narrative.
5. Functional is better than chronological.
6. Neat and thoughtful is better than sloppy and rushed.
7. Truth is always better than fiction.
8. **And never send one without a cover letter.**

23 Avenues

Job hunters are not limited to just one way of job hunting. We have identified 23 different sources for finding jobs, with perhaps more still untapped, that have worked for people when job hunting:

1. Person who leaves (the job and tells you)
2. Competition
3. Employee of the organization/internal move or promotion
4. Suppliers or customers of the organization
5. Unsolicited approach (letter, telephone, cold calls)
6. Schools, colleges, universities, training centers, etc.
7. Employment wanted ads
8. Banks, service organizations, etc.
9. Recruiting agencies, headhunters
10. Friends, contacts, clubs, associations, alumni, others
11. Employment offered ad
12. Official placement agencies (government)
13. Chambers of commerce/professional associations
14. Exhibitions, symposiums, trade shows
15. Job fairs or career conferences
16. Internet – job posting sites (Monster, CareerBuilder, etc.)
17. Internet – job offer listings
18. Internet – company website posts own job listing
19. Former professors or teachers

20. Cultural/spiritual/political groups
21. Temporary employment agencies
22. Company bulletin board, newsletter – internal posting
23. Company calls you

Job hunters can take heart and find comfort in the fact that they are not limited to just one way of job hunting. Certain strategies or sources work better for certain people. Some people are pros at talking with other people to find out information and job leads. Others feel intimidated by such an approach and prefer to respond to employment ads. Some people love to attend trade shows and network for job leads. Others prefer to use the services of headhunters or recruiting agencies. Luckily for all of us, there are choices.

While some job hunters may try to use all of these strategies in one job search, you may want to use three to five.

Take a moment to look over this list and identify the three to five job hunting strategies you would like to integrate into your job search. Whatever strategies you undertake, you must give them your best effort if you are to be successful.

> While we don't recommend a job hunter try to use all of these strategies in one job search, it is possible to try between three to five avenues, without spreading yourself too thin.

While it would be helpful to cover all 23 sources in depth, each one could stand alone and be worthy of its own book. Instead we are focusing on the strategies of Responding to Employment Ads and Using the Unsolicited Approach. Most important of all, we focus on how to write letters that will stand out from the crowd of other candidates.

How Many Different Job Hunting Letters Are Used?

When you understand the job hunting process involves more than just sending a resume to an employer, you will also understand that many different kinds of letters might be necessary during a job search. We have identified on the following chart a list of different letters that are used in job hunting. While it's unlikely that any job hunter would use all of these letters, it's helpful to think about the different scenarios that might occur in a job hunt and be ready to address each one.

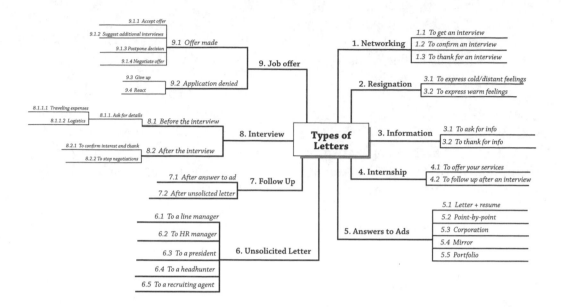

In this book, we will concentrate on the categories of "Answers to Ads" and "Unsolicited Letter."

Make it your mission to learn how to write good letters. The extra time it takes is worth the investment in your future. These letters are used at the beginning of a job contact when first approaching an employer, and can determine how well you get out of the starting gate and how fast you can finish the race – with the prize of a job! If you don't learn how to write a letter that captures the reader's attention and makes them want to contact you for an interview, you will still be on the track when others have finished the race. Anyone can send only a resume – most people do just that. Very few people send good cover letters along with their resume. You want to be the person who stands out among job hunters. Become a "Resource Person" rather than a "Job-Beggar."

This book will teach you how to write a good cover letter by using a **12-step process** that covers each item in the letter in detail. When you are finished with the book, you will know how to write a letter that is specific to you, to the employer you are contacting, and to the job you want.

We could have filled this book with examples of cover letters that some might try to adapt to their own situation, but we know from experience that never really works well. Instead we have discussed, point by point, each item that needs to be covered in your letter. We've included sample letters for illustration, with the hope that you will understand why copying them won't be in your best interest. It is far better you learn how to write to **any** employer and address their needs and concerns in your own voice. With practice you can master this process and excel in your ability to write letters so it takes less time each time you do it.

The Job Market – What Is It and Where Is It?

We call it the "job market," singular tense, as if it were one entity. But that's not really accurate. The job market is made up of **two** markets. There is the "Open Market," where job openings are advertised in traditional channels and job hunters are invited to apply for those jobs. There's a road map, of sorts, to lead you to places where jobs can be found.

> We call it the job market, singular tense. But that's not really accurate. The job market is made up of **two markets**.

There's also the "Hidden Market," where job openings are not advertised in traditional channels. They exist in the world of work, but you have to go looking for them. That means you have to take a proactive approach and seek out those jobs without benefit of a road map. There is no invitation in, so you have to make an **"unsolicited"** (which according to Webster's means: *given, sent, or received without being requested*) approach. You have to make the map yourself, knowing there are "locations" out there, in the form of jobs.

Together, these two markets are where jobs are found. Each has it benefits and drawbacks. Each has its success stories and each has it share of failures. Ideally, you should investigate both "markets" to understand how to make your approach distinctive and effective so you will end up where you want to be.

Many people begin their job hunt in the Open Market by looking at the want ads, also called:

- classified ads
- job postings
- employment ads
- help wanted ads

They believe the ads are a good place to start because they identify what jobs employers want to fill, even when they don't believe they will ultimately use and/or follow up on those ads. Looking at ads is a gradual first step into the world of job hunting. It is non-threatening and helps begin the process.

So, let's start the discussion by looking at the Open Market.

Chapter 3
The Open Market

I t seems simple enough. The Open Market appears self-explanatory: it is open to everyone. This way of looking for a job is accessible to anyone interested enough to open a newspaper to the want ads or look on the Internet for job postings. Ads for jobs are also found in a variety of other places:

- trade magazines
- professional/specialized publications
- company job listing boards
- bulletin boards in professional associations, colleges, or any public place where people congregate

Everyone is invited to respond to the ad theoretically, although qualifications are supposed to reduce the number of people who do respond.

Employment agencies, governmental programs, and executive search firms are also considered part of the Open Market. They are open to all who are interested, although certain criteria are used to narrow down those who want to use these services.

> Everyone is "invited" to apply and no one has to feel nervous about doing so.

The good news about the Open Market is it's an equal opportunity thing – more like equal interest thing – everyone who is interested is welcome to apply, and everyone has the same chance to find out about the job opening. Everyone is "invited" to apply and no one has to feel nervous about doing so. The need is there and the job hunter knows it, and can then decide if he/she would like to try to fill it.

The not-so-good news is that the best estimates place the Open Market at having only about 15%-25% of all job openings. That means a whopping 75%-85% of job openings are never advertised this way, and most job hunters won't find them unless they take the time and trouble to look for them. That's a big piece of the pie to miss when it comes to job search strategies. Another negative aspect of the Open Market is when jobs are advertised and open to anyone and everyone who cares to look, more people will be after the job. And when we think about the employment numbers game, we know that chances go down when there are more candidates for an employer to consider.

Why Use an Employment Ad?

The Open Market requires that employers tell the world about their job openings. To do this, they advertise, promote, market, announce, and/or publicize a job that needs to be filled in their company. Simple enough.

They usually write an ad describing what they need or want, post it somewhere people will see it, and wait for the response.

Companies used to advertise in traditional places like newspapers and trade journals, but with the advent of the Internet, job listings are now commonplace there as well. The good news for job hunters (and employers too) is that more people will see the ad and respond to it; and the bad news for job hunters (and employers too) is that more people will see the ad and respond to it. The Internet might be the most marvelous tool to come along in a long time (well, ever), when it comes to gathering and disseminating information, but it clogs up the works when it comes to job hunting.

In the past an employer might expect responses from an ad to be somewhere in the range of 50 to 100 people (in larger areas), and now – with Internet postings – those responses can easily reach between 300 and 1,000, sometimes more. Hard to know if that's really better for the job hunter (and the employer too).

Why Do Employers Use Job Ads?

1. Ads are cheap – relatively speaking. They write up the ad and send it to their preferred media for posting. Pay the few bucks and it's out in the world.

2. It's faster than waiting for someone to show up, either someone from within their own ranks or an outsider using his/her contacts.

3. It's often clarifying for the employer to sit down and think through what they need in a specific job, and then put it in writing.

4. It makes rejecting people easier. Rejection, when it has to happen, is much easier to do when you're not looking into the eyes of someone else.

5. It's a good way to find new talent – with hundreds or thousands of possible candidates responding to an ad, the diversity, depth, and breadth of candidate experience and skills increases, and employers can pick and choose who might enhance their workforce.

6. It provides a choice for an employer and takes away the fear of being stuck with only one candidate.

7. It's a win/win for the employer. If the right candidate shows up and gets hired, the employer wins. If the right candidate doesn't show up, the employer gets to start over as if the first search never happened – change a few words, change the location of the advertisement, and begin again. No harm, no foul.

How Do Ads Benefit Job Hunters?

We can see some advantages to using ads for job hunters:

1. Ads are cheap – relatively speaking. For the cost of a newspaper or other publication, job hunters can start to find jobs that might be a good fit, and once hooked up to the Internet, there's no cost to locate thousands (or millions) of jobs.

2. It's fast – find the ad today and apply today. No waiting around for anyone to call you back, as often happens when networking. No visiting companies and/or talking with people in the hope there might be a job opening, either now or in the future.

3. Ads make it easy for a job hunter to find openings (theoretically) by simply looking in any place where ads are often found.

4. Using ads is a universally recognized and accepted method of job hunting. Until about 30 years ago when Richard Bolles and others questioned this method and suggested different ways to approach a job hunt, it was certainly the most common and often only way that people looked for job. Ads invite the job hunter in, and remove any feelings of not being welcome to approach a company. And job hunters presume, even if it turns out different in the end, that a particular job is open – the employer has admitted needing a new employee.

5. It takes the guesswork out of the process. The qualifications and job requirements are listed. You either fit them or you don't. You're either interested or you're not.

6. Ads usually list whom to contact in order to apply for a job. No research, networking, or other method is needed – it's listed right in the ad – no conjecture there.

7. Ads make looking for a job in a different geographical area possible. It's pretty hard to know what's available in a different area if you aren't living there or have strong connections to someone who is living there. Ads fill this gap and allow a person in Phoenix to be connected to jobs in Omaha or Boston instantly.

8. It's a safe way to go if the job you want fits into an easily recognized category such as: accounting, administrative, banking, dental, engineering, financial, health care, insurance, management, manufacturing, sales, travel, and warehouse . . . to name a few.

9. Jobs that are easily labeled, described, and categorized fit the format of an ad best, making it easier for a job hunter to understand job tasks and responsibilities.

10. It's considerably less risky and stressful to respond to an ad than it is to try to find another way in the door of a company. Rejection, when it comes, is much easier to take when you're not looking into the eyes of someone else.

11. For those job hunters who excel at writing and know how to capture the imagination and enthusiasm of others with their words, ads are the way to go.

What Are the Problems With Employment Ads?

With all those seeming advantages, why wouldn't all job hunters want to use ads?

1. **Most people who track these kinds of statistics confirm that employment ads advertise/publicize only about 15%- 25% of all jobs open at any given time.** That means 75-85% of jobs are NOT advertised this way. That's a whole lot of jobs out there that won't be listed in the paper or on the Internet. If job seekers rely on the want ads as their ONLY means of looking for a job, they will be missing loads of opportunities. Additionally, it shows a lack of creativity on the part of job hunters and can cast them as passive and desperate if it is the only job hunting method used.

2. **Many ads are misleading.** Some use what might be called the "Superman" approach. You're asked, in the ad, for superhuman qualifications, like the abilities to stop a speeding bullet with your teeth and leap over tall buildings in a single jump, not to mention changing from one outfit

to another wildly colored one – with a cape, no less – in a phone booth (if you could find one) in four seconds flat. Can't be done by those of us who are mortal. These ads appear to want you to be 20 years old with 30 years of experience!

Employers try this tactic, though, reasoning that if they ask for more than they need or want, they will be sure to get what they do want, which is much less than what's advertised. They will be able to narrow down the pool of applicants, as only the bravest and strongest will apply.

On the flip side of that coin is the "Less is More" approach to ads used by employers that list only a one- or two-line job description. Applicants are left grasping at straws to figure out what the job duties will be and how to tailor their communication in response to the ad.

3. **Many ads don't really describe what will ultimately be needed to perform the job well.** It's not that the employer is purposely trying to mislead in this instance; it's just that they really don't know what they want until they've gone through the interview process and have refined and re-defined what the job will actually entail. They start out believing they are describing the skills, qualifications, education, and knowledge needed for the job in the ad, but after talking with applicants and their own staff, they realize that what they advertised for and what they really want are two different things.

4. **Ads work best for positions that are either of a very technical nature, where it's easiest to categorize and define very specific skills and knowledge, or for jobs requiring less sophisticated skills and experience that an employer knows will be gained over time with training once a person is actually in the job.** These last jobs usually appeal to more applicants because they are not so rigid and defined and, therefore, more people feel they have the qualifications needed to apply.

For people looking for the top 5% of jobs in both salary and highly defined skill sets, the want ads are virtually useless. When they exist, many are only posted to fulfill Equal Employment Opportunity Commission (EEOC) or other internal advertising regulations and are generally filled through contacts or by legitimate headhunters.

5. **Applicants need to be careful about what are called "blind ads."** The term "blind ad" refers to an ad that doesn't list a company's name or contact person, but instead asks the applicant to respond to a unnamed P.O. Box (in the case of snail mail), or doesn't allow the applicant to see what email address their response will go to (in the case of email). Many companies use blind ads so they won't be overwhelmed with calls and letters from hundreds or thousands of applicants, and the jobs they advertise are legitimate – they actually do exist. The difficulty arises when

unethical headhunters wishing (and fishing) to fill up their contact databases with names place blind ads. These ads are not for the benefit of job hunters, and it is often very difficult to know the difference between the two. Additionally, if you happen to be an employed person looking for a job and don't want your boss to know, responding to a blind ad often opens a can of worms in ways never anticipated or desired, if you happen to respond to ad placed by your own employer.

6. **The current thinking that the Internet, with its millions and millions of employment ads, is manna from heaven and will end any need to use other avenues to look for work is just plain wrong.** It's true there are job listings to be found. It's true there are even job scouting programs which will search through those millions of jobs and deliver the best ones right to your mailbox. But statistics (from those who keep track of such things) about the effectiveness of this method are NOT in favor of the job hunter. The percentage of people who actually will find a job from a listing on the Internet range in the 4-5% category, broadly speaking (technical jobs fare slightly better at about 10%). That means 90-96% of all people DON'T find a job this way. Out of 100 people, 90 to 96 will be unsuccessful.

   In addition to that abysmal number of failures, job hunters are fooling themselves into thinking that their efforts are productive. They believe they are doing the right thing by spending their time and energy responding to these listings. They aren't, and when they wonder why they haven't gotten one response to the 500 resumes they've sent out over the Internet, it's hard to offer positive affirmation for this method of job hunting.

7. **When jobs are advertised, every person who is interested enough can find them.** There's no way to limit the job's exposure. So the 1,000 other people, with as good a background and personality as yours, are welcome to apply. Your odds go down automatically. It's akin to a lottery where chance defines outcome. It is wiser to use a highly defined tactical approach for a better outcome.

8. **The biggest problem with employment ads is that the whole process is about paper meeting paper.** There is no human contact in any of it, and because there's no real connection it is only acceptable, and not exceptional, as a form of job hunting.

When you do use ads, however, you must do it in a way that will make you stand out among others and offer you the best chance to be interviewed and ultimately hired.

Chapter 4
Using the Want Ads

W hen responding to an employment ad, it is important to familiarize yourself with the language of ads. This helps you understand how to frame your response. It's a good idea to spend some time studying ads in your local paper or on the Internet to see how different companies advertise. Some companies will put lots of information in an ad, and others only one line, leaving you to guess what the job entails. The more you understand the "language" of ads, the better you will do once you actually begin your job hunt.

> Some companies will put lots of information in an ad, and others one line, leaving you to guess what the job entails.

Most printed job ads follow a similar formula, if not in the order of things listed, at least in the categories of information listed. These ads are usually listed in papers and journals alphabetically by job title.

Most ads include:

- Job title
- Company name or kind of company - a generic description of the company without using the actual name. In some cases the company name/profile is skipped altogether
- Job description – requirements/qualifications and skills needed
- Salary or wage (not listed in all ads)
- Contact information

Internet job postings usually offer more information, as space isn't a defining and limiting factor for the listing. The good news is that these include much more information to help you formulate your response. The bad news is there is much more information that might rule you out if your experience, skills, and qualifications don't match what's given in the listing.

> **Administrative Assistant**
> We are a fast-growing chain of floral stores seeking an admin asst with great computer skills, excellent communication, and the ability to work well under pressure.
> 2-5 years admin experience required.
> F/T position in our corporate office in Anytown, Mon-Fri 8-5. Please send resume to Sue Smith at suesmith@abc.com or fax to 555-123-4567

To familiarize yourself with this "language" of ads, study the paper or Internet and find some jobs that are of interest to you. You can focus on jobs that are only mildly interesting to jobs you might really want. For practice, consider calling a few companies who have listed a phone number in their ad but are short on job details to see if you can get more information. This is often called "diffusing" the ad or "upgrading" the ad. If you feel shy about this kind of exercise, start with ads that only mildly interest you. Then if you make a mistake or don't feel you come across well on the phone, you won't lose much and the practice will allow you to get better each time you do it. You can also ask a friend to call for you, since they won't be as emotionally involved and are likely to be less nervous.

> Be prepared, listen, and take notes if you can, and ALWAYS thank them for their time.

Be sure to write down some questions before you ever pick up the phone. It's easiest to start with common kinds of questions, such as:

- *What kind of person are you looking to hire?*
- *What does the job involve?*

and then move on to more specific job content ones, like:

- *Can you tell me the three most important skills you would expect the right candidate to have?*
- *Can you tell me the three most important tasks to be carried out in this job?*
- *What kind of minimum education and training would you expect the candidate to have?*

When you do this, you should be organized and have some pointers in front of you in case you get nervous during the call. Don't waste time – either yours or the people you contact. Be prepared, listen, and take notes if you can, and always thank them for their time.

The more you do this, the better you will get at it and over time, when the job you really want to try for comes along, you will be able to elicit more information than other candidates and then tailor your letter in response to the ad.

Even when you've practiced how to get the information you need to respond to an ad, and have written a good cover letter to accompany your resume or application, you are still facing strong competition that lessens the effectiveness of this strategy of job hunting. It's difficult to know exactly how many responses are generated from a single ad; figures vary from 5 to 3,000, with the majority of ads generating between 100 to 250 applicants. With the rise in Internet responses these numbers may be skewed forever more – since job hunters saturate employers with electronic resumes, ad nauseam.

What's a much more useful and enlightening number to know is that the rate of effectiveness for this method of job hunting hovers between 7 and 24%. Experts put the number of interviews generated by responding to ads at only seven interviews for every 100 responses to an ad. That means out of 100 people, only seven will get an interview, and even if every one of those was offered a job (which is not likely), that's still 93 people who didn't get an interview or job using this method of job hunting. As jobs move up in position, prestige, and salary, the success rate for this method falls. So, you can see how important it is, with statistics stacked against you like this, to make sure you up the odds in your favor.

> As jobs move up in position, prestige, and salary, the success rate for this method falls.

If ads and other avenues on the Open Market only account for 15-25% of all jobs, where are the other 75-85% of jobs to be found?

If you want to venture out another way in your job-hunting activities, you must tap into the Hidden Market.

Chapter 5

The Hidden Job Market

Before we start our discussion about the Hidden Market and the Unsolicited Approach, let's try a little quiz. Look at these 16 questions and circle the answer you think most correct for each question. After you're done with the quiz, go to Appendix C to check how you did. The rationale for each answer is listed there.

Writing and Sending Unsolicited Letters

1. If you have the choice, you use:
    A. The recipient's title rather than their name.
    B. The recipient's name rather than their title.

2. You include:
    A. The names of your previous employers, the titles of your previous jobs, the dates, and periods.
    B. Examples of your achievements, results, and evidence.

3. You send your letter to:
    A. Whomever is most appropriate.
    B. The Personnel Department, or to whoever is responsible for recruitment.

---

4. You start your letter by:

    A. Briefly introducing yourself.

    B. My mentioning a subject/issue which affects the organization or recipient.

5. You think that it is worthwhile:

    A. To include a self-addressed envelope for their answer.

    B. Not to include a self-addressed stamped envelope for their answer.

6. In your letter, you specify that you are looking for a:

    A. Job.

    B. 20-minute meeting.

7. With your cover letter, you should:

    A. Include your resume.

    B. Not include your resume.

8. In your letter, you should describe yourself in:

    A. Great detail

    B. Two or three lines, using information which may be of interest.

9. If the person whom you want to meet is very important:

    A. You approach them directly.

    B. You approach them, for the first time, via their secretary/assistant.

10. Your letters should be:

    A. Handwritten.

    B. Typed.

11. If you don't get an answer:

    A. You don't bother to follow up.

    B. You follow up systematically.

12. The content of a spontaneous letter should be in the following order:
    A. "Me," "you," then "we."
    B. "You," then "me," then "we."

13. In your letter:
    A. You use the word "if" fairly often.
    B. You never use the word "if."

14. To really convince them:
    A. You specify everything you could unquestionably do for them.
    B. You carefully and modestly say what you could do for them.

15. The opening of your letter is written in such a way that it:
    A. Introduces the rest of your letter.
    B. Will not be thrown away by the reader.

16. Of the three parameters – appearance, recipient, and offer:
    A. Appearance is the most important
    B. Recipient is the most important.

The Hidden Market and the Unsolicited Approach

If you rely only on the Open Market during your job hunt, you will miss a huge segment of possible jobs. Understanding that the Open Market is only part of the job market is helpful since that knowledge will allow you to expand your efforts using other strategies if responding to ads doesn't happen to work for you. It's also helpful to know that just because you don't see an ad for the job you want, doesn't mean that job doesn't exist. You don't have to set your sights on some other job that doesn't thrill you nearly as much, if you understand that the Hidden Market is out there and just waiting for you. It's like an ancient castle buried under centuries of dirt. We know it's there; we just have to dig out the buried treasure!

Because by definition, the Hidden Market is "hidden," the job hunter has to uncover it. It will not miraculously show up without effort – it must be uncovered. Simply put, the Hidden Market is the job market that exists **at all times** but doesn't get advertised through traditional means. There are always jobs to be found in the Hidden Market, but the job hunter must go after them – there's no road map to point them out.

It is estimated by experts that at any given time, the majority of companies will have a need to hire roughly 10% more employees. But they don't have the time or resources to launch an ad campaign.

Imagine this: You're a department head, already working 55+ hours a week trying to keep your head above water. You need another employee. You know, to get that employee, you will have to:

1. Write a job description (after consulting with other employees to make sure you have thought of everything).
2. Have HR, legal, or someone higher up approve the ad.
3. Place the ad in one to five publications.
4. Collect and review all 200 applications/resumes that come in for the job (low estimate on that number!).
5. Select the best 15- 20 candidates to invite for an interview after reviewing all the "paper."
6. Call and arrange those interviews (or direct someone else to do it who knows your busy and ever-changing schedule).
7. Interview 5-10 people.
8. Narrow it down to 3-5 candidates.
9. Interview again with those candidates and your superior or others.
10. Select one and make a job offer.
11. Handle a salary negotiation meeting.

If we look at the time these 11 steps might take, it's something like this:

1. 30 minutes to 2 hours
2. 30 minutes (probably have to try 2 or 3 times)
3. 60 to 90 minutes placing ad (which costs money)
4. 3 hours and 20 minutes if only 1 minute per application
5. 30 to 60 minutes
6. 2 hours plus, having to make 15 to 30 calls and re-calls to connect

7. 5 to 10 hours, if only 1 hour per interview
8. 1 hour if not seeing candidates again; 3 to 5 hours if seeing them again
9. 5 to 8 hours; interviews are longer this time
10. 30 minutes
11. 30 minutes

If we take the low side of this estimate, that's still at least 23 hours of work for the employer – the high side of the estimate runs up to 38 hours. That's a lot of time to devote to finding someone new when you already are overworked and overstressed!

Then, imagine this: Out of the blue, a person shows up offering their services for the exact job the employer wants to fill. What's going to be more attractive to the employer? In most cases, if the applicant is qualified and enthusiastic, the employer will be delighted and grateful. And will hire a new employee! Not in every case, but many times.

The Good News of the Hidden Market

The good news about the Hidden Market is four-fold.

1. **It's big!** 75-85% of all jobs are to be found in the Hidden Market.
2. **The Hidden Market exists all the time** – 24/7, 365 days a year. There is never a time when jobs aren't available. Every day in thousands of places, jobs open up for one reason or another and are there for the industrious job hunter to find and claim.
3. **The odds are better;** if 2,000 other people aren't trying for the very same job, the person who ferrets out the opening will stand a much greater chance of actually being the one who gets the job. It's the early bird (and in this case, perhaps the only bird) who gets the job.
4. **The job hunter can be as proactive as he/she wants in this "market."** No sitting around waiting for someone to advertise a job you want. No scattergun approach of responding to ads with little or no response from employers.

Some argue the downside of the Hidden Market is the fact that it's so hard to know where to look, when to look, how to look, and whom to contact. That's true. It requires work, imagination, and grit on the part of the job hunter, and maybe a thick skin to deal with the "no's" before getting to the "yes." But when put into perspective, that what's expected once you get a job – work! Better results for better effort.

Perhaps the greatest obstacle to the Hidden Market is that many job hunters are terribly uncomfortable showing up, in paper form and especially in person, to an employer "uninvited." Job hunters fear the employer will usher them to the door, hang up the phone on them, or toss their letters and resumes into the basket, without ever giving them a chance. They reason if the employer had a job they wanted filled, they would advertise it. Well, maybe. But experience shows that's just not the case at least 75-85% of the time!

> You must do the legwork, homework, and just plain work of finding the job you want.

Tapping into the Hidden Market means using an "unsolicited" approach – taking the initiative to find a job when you haven't been invited in, by way of an ad. You must do the legwork, homework, and just plain work of finding the job you want.

If you can learn to love the Hidden Market and use it every time you think about changing jobs or look for another job, you will be ahead of the game. It is usually your best chance to find the job you want, particularly when that job doesn't fit into some neat category. Statistics on the success of this method of job hunting jump significantly and run from 33% to 84% (according to *What Color Is Your Parachute?*, 2005 Edition) depending on how you do it. Starting at the lower end of the range and working to the upper end of the range, success increases by:

- asking others about job openings in their companies
- knocking on doors of companies you like
- painstakingly researching companies and jobs and then contacting companies that interest you
- working in groups to research and approach companies

These statistics should make most job hunters jump for joy, knowing they can move from a 7% effectiveness rate when using only ads, to an 84% effectiveness rate when, in the company of others, they research and contact companies they like.

There are, however, three fatal errors when using the unsolicited approach that will drop these success rates, like an anvil falling from a tall building, and cause a job hunter to rightfully think these statistics are false or over-inflated.

Fatal Errors to Avoid

Fatal Error No. 1: *The job hunter will send their letter to the Personnel Department or Human Resources Department, and it will never get to the person who can appreciate what they offer.*

While usually staffed by highly qualified and professional people, these Personnel and H.R. departments have as one of their primary functions the responsibility for screening and hiring, but often don't understand or have the time to value what you are offering. They are so busy dealing with hundreds or thousands of other applicants that your communication is likely to get lost in the fray. It's not that they don't want to help you. It is more probable that they don't always know where to send your letter, which means it goes NOWHERE.

Fatal Error No. 2: *The job hunter will ask for a job instead of asking for a meeting.*

You must always ask for a meeting to discuss further possibilities. Neither side really knows if there is a good match until qualifications, experience, and personalities can be explored. You're jumping the gun here to ask for a job; if you jump too soon, it's more likely you will fail.

Fatal Error No. 3: *The job hunter will send their letter with the very instrument of their elimination: their resume.*

When you send a resume, you send the vehicle most often used to screen people out, rather than in. It is a better strategy to present information about why you have contacted the employer and what you are offering that is specific to them. This kind of approach stands a greater chance to create enough interest in you so the employer will want to learn more by calling you in for a meeting.

When a job hunter makes one or more of these errors, they damage their chance for success in their unsolicited approach.

So, how can a job hunter be successful using this approach?

Learn From the Experts

There is a lot to be learned from the experts who do "mass mailings" and have studied what is most important in an initial contact when sending a written communication. These specialists have determined that the success of any mailing depends on three parameters: R.O.D.

R = **Recipient** - this accounts for 50% the success of your mailing
O = **Offer** (or proposal) – this accounts for 35% the success of your mailing
D = **Design** (or appearance) – this accounts for 15% the success of your mailing

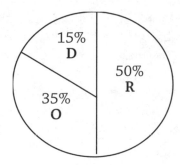

When viewed in this light, it's easy to understand that if your letter doesn't get to the right recipient, your success falls drastically to only 50%, and then only in the best of circumstances.

The "R"

So, who should be the recipient of your letter?

- The person who can best understand the value of your offer
- The person who needs what you can do most
- The person who has the power to hire
- The person who makes decisions about whom to interview
- The Number 1 in a small organization
- The person for whom you would work if hired
- The person who knows your area of specialization well

As you seek to discover who should receive your initial approach, keep in mind the following five principles that can help you get to the right person:

1. Address your letter to the person who can best take advantage of your services.
2. Make sure that what you offer presents absolutely NO risk to the recipient.
3. Find a person in the company or organization who will serve as your "pilot" within that company and lead you to others who can help you.
4. Use your network to find the name(s) of those you should approach.
5. When you do not know to whom to address your communication, aim for a level higher than the one you wish to reach. Messages come down in a company much more easily than they go up. It is much more likely that a V.P. will send your letter down to a Department Manager, than the other way around.

How can you put a name to this person? You can try a variety of ways, including:

1. Looking on the company's website for names. If the person you want to contact isn't listed by title, you may consider contacting someone who is listed and asking them for the name of the person you wish to reach.

2. Contacting people you know that might know someone working at the desired company and asking for a name.

3. Phoning the company directly and asking for the name of the person who is the _____, title of the person you wish to contact — for example, Manager of After-Sales.

4. Calling the company and asking for Accounts Receivable; then asking for the name of the person who is in charge of _____.

5. Calling and asking for the exact spelling of the name of the person who is in charge of _____.

6. Calling and asking for the name of the person who is in charge of _____ and to whom you wish to send a letter which is not urgent but important.

When we learn from professionals in the mailing business, we then understand that the person who is to get the letter is ultimately the most important parameter to success. The recipient is more important than what is said or how the letter looks. You must make sure that your letter goes to the person who will appreciate it most.

The "O"

Once you've identified the correct recipient you must turn your attention to "O," the offer or proposal that makes up the substance of your letter. It isn't sufficient to say that you want to meet them and are interested in their company because you think you will be the solution to their problems!

Never use the word "problems" — they don't have problems, only:

- Challenges to be faced
- Tasks to be carried out
- Opportunities to be seized
- Issues to address
- Resources to be redeployed
- Missions to be achieved

Showing that you understand the issues they are facing, what irritates them or creates anxiety, their recurrent concerns and/or what costs them money or time to fix, can open doors. You must show how you can help meet their needs, with concrete examples and achievements. Offer two or three examples only (keep this brief) of the services you can offer, the tasks you can carry out, or your ideas for the specific resolution of an issue facing them.

> You must show how you can help meet their needs, with concrete examples and achievements.

You must also ask for a short meeting and not a job! Suggest who should be responsible for follow-up. You will use this meeting, if granted, to develop the points in your letter and answer any other questions they might have about you.

The "D"

The final aspect of your letter, "D" for design, carries less weight than the first two parameters, but should still be given proper attention and care. Your letter is not the place to experiment with zany styles. You must use a standard business format for your letter and make sure your grammar, punctuation, and spelling are correct. Do not make even one typo!

You stand a much better chance for success when you address all three parameters of your letter correctly.

However:

- If you send your letter to the right recipient, with an interesting offer, but your design is mediocre, your chances diminish.

- If you send your letter to the right recipient, with an appealing design, but your offer is mediocre, your chances diminish.

- If you send your letter to the wrong recipient, with an interesting offer and a wonderful design, your chances diminish.

All three parameters matter, regardless of the percentage of importance. Missing by 15% is still enough reason to eliminate your letter. If you don't get the elements right in any area, that element suddenly jumps to the forefront in the mind of the person who gets your letter. Take care with every part of your letter.

Try a Call

If you want to contact a company and know the person you wish to reach, consider calling them and just talking to them, one human being to another. Tell them of your interest, why you've called, and one or two things about your experience and achievements – be brief – and if they show interest in you (their tone of voice, questions, and comments will speak to their interest), ask for a short meeting to explore possibilities. You might be surprised at how many people will be friendly and open to your approach. This seems particularly true as you move up in professional status and salary. Don't rule this out because you feel nervous. Know what you want to say before you call, don't waste anyone's time, and you might be delighted at the results. What's the worst that can happen?

Chapter 6

Increasing the Odds

L et's look at job hunting as a time-motion study. There are just so many minutes in a day a person can spend on job hunting activities. What activity the job hunter chooses determines how those minutes get used. Time can be spent answering ads, writing letters and resumes, making phone calls, visiting with contacts, reading books on the subject, surfing the Internet, building a network, contacting alumni and service organizations, working with career counselors, attending trade fairs, and so on.

Every minute used for one activity cannot be used for another. So, if a job hunter chooses to use the time surfing the Internet instead of responding to ads or making a call, that time is gone and can't be called back and re-used for something more fruitful. The smart job hunter wants to be sure to use time wisely – in the way that is most likely to bring the best results.

It may help to look at job hunting activities with the following three criteria:

1. Does it provide a challenge for you?
2. Is it effective (productive)?
3. Does it present a risk of being screened out?

Then it could be asked, *"Is it more challenging, productive, and less risky to spend five hours sending your resume to 200 jobs that might (just maybe) be a match for you (but probably not) on the Internet, thinking that the sheer number of contacts ups your chances for getting an interview?"* That reasoning might hold up if it weren't that 200,000 other people were also doing the same thing.

"Is it more challenging, productive and less risky to craft five well thought-out letters (and matching resumes) and send them to five companies you had researched after calling to find the name of the correct person to contact?"

"Is it more challenging, productive, and less risky to spend five hours meeting with people you know who work at companies that are of significant interest to you?"

Since the same amount of time is used for all three options, which is likely to bring the best result? The trick to successful job hunting is to use your time wisely and in ways that have been proven to get results.

You may want to apply the following matrix to your job hunting activities:

Job Hunting Method Used	Challenging	Efficiency	Risk Involved (of being screened out)
Answering an ad	No	7%	High
Unsolicited letter	Somewhat	40 to 60%	Medium to low
Personal contact	Very	50 to 70%	Low

Do Your Homework Well

It takes some time – not a lot once you get going – to write a letter to someone you don't know asking to be considered for a meeting, which is what a good cover letter should do – ask for a meeting, NOT a job. Spending the time to find out something about the company or person you are writing to will be worth your effort, especially when you know that by doing so you can raise your chances of your letter being read. This person might be the one who will make the decision about whom to interview or hire, and they can see the value in your extra effort. A few extra minutes of your time might mean the difference in an extra minute or two of their time while they read your letter. It's a good trade-off! When you spend more time to make sure your first contact is the best you have to offer, the results will be better, too.

> If spending an hour researching a company before writing a cover letter isn't worth the time, please stop and consider if you really want the job.

If you feel that spending an hour researching a company/industry/recipient or job content before trying to write your cover letter isn't worth the time, **please stop and consider if you really want the job.** If you aren't willing to take the time to do this step, it might be a sign that your heart's not really in it.

You might also think, "*Well, if I have to research every job I want to apply for, I will only be able to send a few applications/letters a day.*" It's true you won't be able to blanket the Internet with your resume this way, but compare results from that strategy – sending your resume blindly to any job that looks like it might even remotely match you in some way – to sending a well-crafted letter and tailored resume which specifies exactly when you will be following up to set a meeting time. If you like the results from the first strategy, keep doing it. If you don't like the results, you must move to the strategy of doing your homework first if you don't want to keep getting the same results.

So, what does that mean to the job hunter?

It means your first contact shouldn't be all about you. While you're an interesting topic, no doubt, most employers don't want to feel you've picked them out of the Yellow Pages and find them no more special than the next listing. Even were that the case, don't let them think that you couldn't be bothered to find out something about their company or business.

It means taking time to do some homework. When you find a job that's interesting to you, no matter how you find it (through ads, contacts, cold calling, etc.), find out something **more** about the company, field, job specifics, and/or the person who you should contact. The Internet has made this kind of research a snap now. Most companies with over five employees have a website. And for those without access to the Internet, there are more traditional ways to gather information.

It means you should tell the employer you know something about them. You focus on their concerns and needs, and not your own.

If you think that sounds like work, it is. But let's put it in perspective – how much time would you spend to research a new car if you were interested in buying it?

- Would you spend five or ten minutes checking out what *Consumer Reports* or *Kelley Blue Book* had to say?

- Would you spend five or ten minutes looking at the specifications and details on the manufacturer's website?

- Would you spend five or ten minutes talking with someone who already had the car to get their feedback?

- Would you make a trip to the car lot to look it over and get a brochure to study, at the very least?

Most people would. All that effort for something that costs money! And once you decided you were interested you would probably do it fast to get your answer.

Keep that idea in mind when you begin to research a job. Give it at least the effort you would give researching a car. If you do this kind of thing for every job that really interests you, you will accomplish at least four very important things.

1. You will hone your research skills and become much better at it as you go along, allowing you to spend less time doing it.

2. You will learn and begin to understand key terms. This is especially helpful if you are making a radical career change. When the time comes, you will be able to speak the "specific industry language" which gives you immediate credibility.

3. You will build your confidence to answer the question, when you make it to the meeting stage, "Why did you pick our company – what about us interests you?"

4. All information gained is useful – if not for the particular job you have in mind now, then for something else down the road. All information is a springboard to other information. All contacts you make in the process are important. The person you talk with today could be the person who is in a position to hire you tomorrow. By showing your initiative and enthusiasm now, you will stand out later on.

Know Your Target

It's impossible to write a good letter if you don't know what you are talking about! BEFORE putting one word down on paper, you must do some research on:

- the industry/field
- the company
- the job content
- the person you are contacting

The Industry

The easiest place to start your research is with the field or industry. Spend some time getting an overview of the field to find out:

- Significant trends and current events affecting the industry
- Technological advances
- Recent transactions and business changes – companies sold and/or acquired by others

- Jargon and business terms germane to the field
- Hiring practices and qualifications
- Industry leaders
- Industry events such as trade shows and fairs
- Copyrights and trademarks
- Legal and regulatory issues
- Industry journals and publications

When you have done your research, you will have useful background information that can help you as you apply for one or more jobs in that field.

Try this game. Pretend you're a detective and someone asked you to tell them five different things about the industry/field you are investigating that were unique and interesting. Let's say they wanted to know:

- the name of the most widely read trade publication
- the most recent patent obtained in the field
- the name of the five largest companies (either in number of employees or revenue) and the names of their CEOs
- the next trade show in your area
- what one single event or product had most changed the industry in the last year or two

Start your quest on the Internet (if you have access) and keep track of how many sites it takes you to get this information. See if one site might be able to answer all the questions. See how many layers you have to click through on any given site to find an answer to one or more of your questions. Follow the trail of sites that lead you deeper to the answers. See how creative you can be to get the information you want. If and when you run into roadblocks, figure ways to get around them. Keep track of information you learn that doesn't answer your five questions, but tells you something else important about the industry. When you do get the information you want, congratulate yourself on your superior sleuthing skills and then put the information to good use in your job search.

Just as examples:

- When we typed "Photo Industry" into Google, over 98 million listings came up. Within the first few listings was a site for one of the industry's popular trade publications, which listed a calendar of trade shows and information on some of the newest products. This took less than two minutes to do.

- When we typed "Biking + Food" into Clusty, over 800,000 listings came up. We found the listings of several companies that produce and sell food for biking trips.

- When we typed "Bioengineer + Soil" into Clusty, over 1,900 listings came up. We found the listing of a very prominent scientist working in this field and his lab page explaining opportunities with his company.

- When we typed in "Writer + Magazines" into Ask.com, over 3 million listings came up. There were dozens of sites that outlined the process for writing and submitting articles, and many magazines had their own sites detailing their submission requirements.

The Internet allows anyone, anytime, to research just about anything. Start by using any search engine (Google, Yahoo, MSN, Netscape, Ask.com, Clusty, Lycos, Iwon, AOL Search, Altavista, Go (formerly Infoseek), ICQ, – there are hundreds of them) and type in the name of the field you want to research. You'll be amazed by the numbers of listings that pop up, when you first start this kind of research. Don't worry, you don't need to look at them all! You can look over the top 20 listings that come up and start by clicking on any one of interest. When you find a site with some pertinent information, continue to drill down into that site for more helpful information. Keep clicking through each site until you feel you have gained some useful information and want to go to another site to learn something else.

If you happen to be someone who doesn't have a computer or know how to use one, you can go to any large public library and use their computer and printed research materials. It will take much longer to find information using printed materials, but it can be done. Most libraries have well-trained and creative research librarians who can point you in the right direction if you tell them what you want to know. They are a valuable resource for you. Also, visit the One-Stop Career Center nearest you for your online job search assistance.

The Company

When you have obtained some meaningful information and have a better understanding of the forces at work in your chosen industry, move the focus of your research to investigating those companies that interest you. If you are responding to an ad, you might already have the name of the company you need to research, if it was listed in the ad. If you are trying an unsolicited approach and don't have any specific companies in mind yet, use the Internet or Yellow Pages to identify a few in your area, or the area you wish to work if you are contemplating a geographical move. There are many, many books and guides that detail company information. To name only a few:

- *American Big Businesses Directory - Company/Industry Section*
- *American Manufacturers Directory*
- *America's Corporate Families*
- *Corporate Directory of U.S. Public Companies*
- *Corporate Yellow Book*
- *Directory of American Firms Operating in Foreign Countries*
- *D&B Business Rankings*
- *D&B Directory of Service Companies*
- *FaxUSA*
- *Harris New England Manufacturers Directory*
- *Hoover's Handbook of American Business*
- *Hoover's Handbook of Private Companies*
- *Hoover's Handbook of Emerging Companies*
- *Hoover's Masterlist of U.S. Companies*
- *Interstate Manufacturers and Industrial Directory, Buyers Guide*
- *Manufacturing & Distribution U.S.A.*
- *Million Dollar Directory*
- *Reference Book of Corporate Managements*
- *Standard and Poor's 500 Guide*
- *S & P MidCap 400 Directory*
- *Standard & Poor's Register of Corporations, Directors and Executives*
- *Walker's Manual of Unlisted Stocks*
- *Ward's Business Directory*

Additionally, most states have their own directories – often more than one – that can help the job hunter research companies. Many libraries have these directories, as they are usually too costly for most individuals to buy, and make them available for the general public to use.

Information you might look for on a company includes:

- The company's main product or service
- Secondary products or services
- Leadership - try to find out CEO, CFO, COO, and board members (if applicable)
- Major customers, clients, suppliers, vendors
- History
- Recent transactions
- New developments
- Number of employees and locations
- Hiring practices
- Competitors
- Annual and quarterly reports for review

- Mentions in the press
- Awards and recognition
- Earnings and current stock price (if publicly traded company)
- Mission statement

When researching a company, begin by checking if it has a website. As with researching an industry or field, you can use a search engine (like Google) and type in the name of the company. If it's a common name you can narrow down your search by typing the name of the company, the plus sign (+), and the location of the company.

For example, you could type into Google:

ABC Graphic Arts + Arizona

If you know the city, use it to further narrow down the search:

ABC Graphic Arts + Phoenix + Arizona

The more specific the parameters you list when using a search engine to find something, the easier and faster you will find what you're looking for. If, at first, you don't come up with the information you want, try approaching it another way. Search for the name of the owner or president if you know it, or search for the type of business (in this example you could put in "graphic arts companies + Phoenix). Remember, the more general your parameters, the more listings you will have to look through to get the information you really want.

> The more general your parameters, the more listings you will have to look through.

When you find the website for a company, read through the entire site, taking notes as you go and jotting down questions that occur to you. Be sure to read articles about the company in magazines, newspapers, and other media. Print out the articles if you can, to refer back to, or even consider sending with your letter to show the sincerity of your interest and enthusiasm for the company.

Many companies will send their annual report and other printed materials (brochures and promotional literature) if you ask. If you call to get this material, ask the person you speak with about the company in a friendly and non-threatening way, if it feels appropriate. You might find you get some firsthand information this way.

Play the detective game again and see if you can uncover five interesting facts about the company. When you feel you have thoroughly researched a company well enough to talk with someone else about it in an intelligent way, consider yourself armed with enough information to contact them. This research will help you decide if you are really attracted to the company, if what you find out makes you more interested, rather than less interested.

If you are responding to an ad where you know the company's name, your job is easier than if you are doing more general research about where you want to go next and don't have company names. If conducting this kind of search, don't limit yourself to only one company, but try not to spread yourself too thin either. Researching between three and seven companies is plenty to give you a solid base from which to move forward.

The Job Content

After completing your studies on the field/industry and specific company or companies, it's time to further narrow down your research and determine the job content. This investigation will often be the most important research you can do, especially when you don't know exactly what a job entails. Without sufficient criteria about the job content, it's hard to know if the job is right for you.

When responding to a specific ad, some of the duties and requirements may be outlined already but you need to make sure you understand terms. What you might call an "Administrative Assistant" might be what someone else would call a "Marketing Coordinator."

For job content, you need to define, in concrete terms, attributes that you possess and want to use in your job and then match it with the job advertised:

- transferable skills
- duties/tasks
- responsibilities
- job functions
- education
- training
- special knowledge
- personal characteristics (personality traits)

 A great benefit about the Internet in this regard is that job listings are often very detailed and descriptive and will allow you to fully understand the job content required. Make a list of at least 10 to 12 items about a job that you can clearly define as a match to your skills, and background. It is in this way you can determine if the job content and your qualifications match.

For example, you may discover that you possess, and want to use at your next job, the abilities of synthesizing information, problem solving, communicating ideas clearly, and dealing with complexity and ambiguity. Your social skills may include persuasion, tact, and the ability to motivate and counsel. You may further determine that your self-management skills include initiative, creativity, meticulousness, and stick-to-it-iveness – sometimes called good old persistence! Your educational background includes a degree in Communications and you have attended training in several management workshops. You want to work in the field of Public Relations, concentrating on the broadcasting area. You must use this information to determine if you can match the jobs you want at the companies you are targeting.

You must know what's involved in the job you want and what the job is called. Don't expect an employer to figure it out for you. It's not their job!

When you feel confident that you have enough information about the field/industry, company, and job content, it's time to focus on the name of the person who will be the recipient of your letter.

The Recipient of the Letter

If a name of the person you need to contact is listed on an ad, you are ahead of the game. Make sure this is not the Human Resources or Personnel Department, however. You can look for any person using Google or another search engine, by simply typing in their first name and last name to see if any listings come up.

As an example, when we typed our names into Google, "Frances Bolles Haynes" came back with 10,300 results and "Daniel Porot" came back with 18,000 results. That is a lot of listings, but many of them are redundant or about other people with the same names. The further you go into the listings the less useful they will be. But in those thousands of listings about us, there is information on our writings, activities, interviews we've done, etc. A clever job hunter could read about either one of us and emerge with some information or questions that would be impressive to us and show their interest in our work.

To narrow down the number of listings that are generated, type in the first name (Daniel), then a plus ("+") sign, then the last name (Porot), i.e., Daniel + Porot. You may also use quotation marks around the name "Daniel Porot," to narrow down the listings. This will eliminate any listing with just the name Daniel or any listing with just the name Porot from appearing – reducing from 18,000 to 11,000 the listings in this example.

If the person you are looking for isn't in the "public eye," there is still a good chance they might be found this way. When we searched for a friend of ours who owns a small graphic design company in Orange County, California, we got 323 results for his name.

Try this exercise every time you know the name of the person you want to contact or, if you've made it to the interview stage, the name of the person who will be interviewing you. It only takes few seconds and you might find out some useful information.

If nothing is listed for the person you want to contact, check out someone else in the company. This information might prove helpful down the road and may end up useful in your job search.

If it turns out you just can't find out the name of, or anything else about, the person you are interested in contacting, you will have to proceed with only the information you have discovered about the field/industry, company, and job content and title. While we've told you that it makes a big difference in the success rate (50%) of an initial contact to know the name of the person who can best appreciate what you have to offer, sometimes it just isn't possible to get this information (without hiring a detective). In these rare cases, move ahead anyway as the research you have done will be more than most other job hunters have done, and will show your interest and enthusiasm for the job. It's not the best scenario, but moving forward is better than doing nothing.

This kind of up-front research and analysis will put you ahead of the majority of job hunters, who, much to our disappointment and their chagrin, don't take the time to make a proper, and hence successful, approach. Mass mailing resumes to hundreds of companies isn't the way to go! It's ineffective and wastes everybody's time and energy. We understand when this is done it helps a job hunter feel like they have done something productive. But the truth is, the time would be much better spent doing research that refines and targets companies and jobs that fit what you really want. When this is done and followed by thoughtful consideration of how to marry the company's needs (and not your own) with your suitability for the job, the results are positive.

Chapter 7
Sensitive Issues

W e've mentioned the real barriers that stand in the way of many job hunters at the beginning of this book, and what can be done about them. It would be naïve, however, to suggest that job hunters don't face very real sensitive issues sometimes in the job-hunting process. In most cases, the sensitivity of these issues has more to do with the perceptions and feelings of the employer or person holding the power to hire, than they do with the person applying for a job, whether responding to an ad or using an unsolicited approach.

It would be great if every job hunter had a stellar career history with no missteps or problems. No job hunter would ever have to worry whether all ethnic, religious, or economic groups were treated the same. How nice it would be if no one cared if you were fired, were a job-hopper, were brand-new to the workforce, were over 50, or had served time in jail or prison.

> Every job hunter must find ways to overcome obstacles by understanding the fears that lie beneath them.

Finding a job would be a snap for all of us if that were the case. We'd never feel insecure about a sensitive issue or need to wonder if disclosing some "hiccup" or more serious issue in our past would cost us the chance to get the job we wanted.

Since we don't live in Xanadu or some other utopia or paradise where life is fair and everyone gets what they want, we have to deal with it. We live in a real world with real problems, some of which are ours.

The good news (or bad, depending on your point of view) is that almost every person who looks for a job faces sensitive issues, obstacles, or objections that have to be overcome. Some are more apparent than others, but we all have at least three to five different "disabilities" in the eyes of others, that create reasons why we might not be the candidate of choice for any given employer. This exists regardless of whether we like it, it's fair or unfair, it breaks job-discrimination laws and flies in the face of political correctness. These factors exist and are acted upon every day.

That means that every job hunter must find ways to overcome these obstacles by understanding the fears that lie beneath them.

When a job hunter is able to understand the objections an employer might have to hiring a person with any one of the many issues faced by each and every person, they are equipped to deal with an objection up front. These fears, usually born of inexperience with someone who has the issue, or born of ignorance, can be laid to rest.

In many cases (but not all), what is most important isn't actually the trait or characteristic or disability that might be objectionable to an employer, but how the job hunter describes the ways they are dealing with the perceived inadequacy/ deficiency/lack/disability/problem.

The decisions and choices each person makes regarding how they meet obstacles and challenges, whether about themselves or others, speaks volumes about who the person is and how successful they will be in life.

It's important to understand the difference between "diversity" sensitive issues and "physical, emotional, and mental disabilities" sensitive issues. **There is a very real difference between the two – both practically and perceived**. Diversity issues include factors that are usually perception preferences – such as gender, age, ethnic origin, and religious affiliation; they are part of who you are but may not necessarily and usually don't impact how you do your job. They are issues that a potential employer might base decisions on about whom to hire or not hire (no matter if illegal or discriminatory), but these factors don't limit your ability to do any particular job.

"Physical, emotional, and mental disabilities" sensitive issues are a different thing. These kinds of issues are generally more apt to limit what a person can do in one or more areas. Based on the nature of the disability, a person may be precluded from doing certain jobs, but not all jobs. A physical or mental disability might make it impossible for a person to do jobs beyond the scope of their abilities, but most people with these disabilities can do some kind of a job. For example, a person who has suffered a spinal cord injury and uses a wheelchair is not going to be a messenger running packages from floor to floor in a high-rise office building. They could however, be the perfect person to answer phones and route calls to their proper locations.

In these cases, it is essential that the job hunter clearly identifies and accepts their limitations, needs, and abilities. They must understand and accept what they can and cannot do and not expect that an employer won't be sensitive to that too. They must know if the job they want to do will require some kind of an accommodation that an employer can make. When they know this, they can deal with these issues and move forward with their job hunt, secure in the knowledge that they will be able to show an employer their value.

You might feel, *"It's a little naïve to think that every person with a prejudice, bias, or preconceived notion is going to let go of it, just because I can show them why it doesn't matter to my job performance."* You'd be right to be skeptical. Sometimes a job hunter will come up against a person during the job hunt whose bias is appalling, unethical, and irrelevant. Those people do exist and you know immediately you don't want to work for them, regardless of whether they would actually hire you. That's understandable and probably prudent. The only problem is, they might hold the key for entrance into an organization that has the job you really want and are qualified for. What should be considered then is how much their attitude would impact you if you were to be hired. Would you be working directly for them or would it be someone else? If they are only the ticket in, and not the person to whom you would report, consider whether you want to tell them to take a hike – even if you'd be entirely justified. Do you throw away the baby with the bath water? Maybe yes, maybe no. Depends on your end goal.

How to Deal With a Sensitive Issue

Give some realistic thought to the areas in your life, both personal and professional, that might cause you problems with a potential employer. Think about the things that you control and could deal with, so that they won't be barriers to employment. Don't be defensive. It's true an employer might not have a right to reject you based on a sensitive issue, but if they keep doing it, it is up to you to change the outcome by changing how you view the problem and how you deal with it. Perhaps there are things you would like to shore up or undertake as a new goal to gain skills? Put in place a strategy/plan to overcome your deficiency and reach your new goal. Then you can honestly answer any questions that come your way and prove to be obstacles to finding a job. You won't have to feel uncomfortable or threatened by these issues.

> Put in place a strategy to overcome your deficiency and reach your new goal.

These issues as they affect a job hunter, whether caused by personal weak points, membership in a specific minority, or job or career missteps, can be looked at in three different ways:

1. **The Legal Aspect**

    Each country has its own guidelines about what can legally be asked during a hiring interview. Some issues, if raised, could make it unlikely that a candidate would be hired. This has necessitated the need for guidelines to protect people from unfair hiring practices. For instance, in the United States it is illegal for an interviewer to ask questions about, or discriminate on the basis of, age, gender, religious preference, or ethnic group.

2. **The Ethical Aspect**

    Every job hunter has to deal with their own conscience. It is never a good policy to bluff or lie when job hunting, even if you have had trouble spots in your past. It is always better to deal with the issues straightforwardly. If you do lie or bluff, you will likely pay for it later, and the consequences will be much greater than if you had dealt with the issue immediately and straightforwardly. The best way to avoid the need for bluffing or lying is to adopt a smart strategy to deal with your issue.

3. **The Strategic Aspect**

    Careful consideration and reflection about sensitive issues are a must for everyone as they prepare for a job hunt, especially when it's time to write their cover letters and resumes, and attend interviews. People must be prepared to deal with any sensitive issue affecting them, to avoid being eliminated by an employer. The job hunter must decide beforehand the attitude to be adopted: Will it be reactive – waiting for the employer to bring up sensitive issues? Or will it be proactive – the candidate approaching and dealing with the issues before an employer brings them up?

Preparation

Determine what sensitive issues might impact a potential employer you want to contact. Determine if the problem is only an inconvenience for the organization you would like to work for. Ask this question of friends and colleagues and consider their opinions. For example, a person who is a diabetic could easily undertake a non-active administrative position. Their health condition would not be a cause for concern in this case.

Prepare Your Scenario

Think about your sensitive issues carefully. Think about how they affect you in your daily life and consider how they might affect a potential employer or their clients or customers, were you to be hired. Spend time preparing strategies on how to handle these issues at any point in your job hunt. Do they need to be addressed in your cover letter? Do they need to be addressed in your resume? Will they come up in an interview? Should they come up in an interview? Practice strategies to deal with any issue you believe could be a trouble spot and figure out when it should be dealt with – up front, in an interview, once hired, or never.

To do this:

- Anticipate all the objections an employer might give regarding your sensitive issues.

- Write out one or two paragraphs of information to have ready to use to explain and refute each objection. This explanation should be only one to two sentences if written, or last only about 20-30 seconds when spoken.

- Practice with a partner each scenario (at least 15 times) until you feel confident and relaxed about the issues. Unless you are relaxed, the employer won't be; you set the tone. The very act of practicing this technique to overcome your sensitive issues allows you to diffuse their impact on prospective employers.

Decide on Your Attitude

When dealing with a sensitive issue, you can adopt one of two attitudes. You can be reactive or proactive.

If you select reactive, you wait for the employer to bring up the subject. Consider that they may not do this, but, rather, just eliminate you from consideration without ever giving a reason why.

Obviously, you will have to deal with any physical issues that are apparent, as they cannot be overlooked. You must prepare your responses only to show how the issue will not be a hindrance to your ability to do the job.

You can choose not to reveal issues that are not visible. At first glance this often seems like a good approach, but usually backfires later if you are offered the job and your employer finds out you have "hidden" information from them. It is best in these cases to quickly discuss it and move on (as late as possible in a meeting after establishing some rapport), proving how it is not a problem with huge consequences for the job you now wish to do.

If you select proactive, YOU initiate discussion of your sensitive issue(s). You can do this:

- at the cover letter stage
- at the beginning of an interview
- during an interview, prior to being offered a job
- during an interview, after a firm job offer has been made
- after an interview, but prior to beginning to work
- during the probationary period
- after the probationary period

When you choose to be proactive, you can:

- choose the best moment to bring up the issue
- demonstrate that you know how to turn what could be perceived as a problem into a potential asset
- prove that your issue will not have repercussions on your ability to function in the job you now wish to do

Choose the Best Time to Reveal Your Issue

We believe it is best, with some exceptions, that a job hunter does NOT announce any sensitive issues prior to an interview. If you decide to reveal a sensitive issue without face-to-face contact, you will be unable to neutralize the effect this might have, and you will likely be screened out before having a chance to get an interview.

The exceptions are when withholding the information would cause the prospective employer to lose any trust they would have in you, and feel betrayed in some way by your omission of a fact that needed to be dealt with before a job could be offered to you.

You can decide to use a cover letter to introduce a sensitive issue, but you run a great risk when you do this. You may find it necessary to address a gap in employment, knowing that if you deal with it in your letter it might allow you to remain in the running for the job. You may find it necessary to disclose the fact that you have been in prison. You may find it necessary to disclose the fact that you have a physical or sensory disability which would be apparent upon meeting you. Choose this option only when you can address your issue succinctly and without emotion in one or two sentences and move on. If your sensitive issue takes a paragraph or two to explain, the letter should NOT be the messenger.

It is important to understand that your best chance of overcoming a sensitive issue is to deal with it face to face in a meeting. Interviewers often look for reasons to screen someone out rather than reasons to include someone. You cannot give all the information about yourself that would prove why you should be hired unless you have enough time. The only way to get that time is during an interview, when you can outline the positive contributions you would make.

Think carefully about your sensitive issues and formulate a strategy early on, on when and how you will deal with them. When you feel confident that you can handle them at any stage in the job hunting process, you will have more confidence in yourself at every stage of the job hunting process!

Chapter **8**
The Purpose of a Cover Letter

Let's be very clear about the purpose of a cover letter. It has one overriding purpose and one overriding purpose only. It is to get a meeting! It is not to get a job. We doubt seriously, although it may have occurred in special circumstances when meeting a candidate is not possible, that many job hunters get a call offering them a job after merely sending a letter and resume. Most employers want to meet with a candidate and get more information and a feel for who the person is – using their intuitive judgment that's based on many things other than employment history – such as appearance, body language, eye contact, punctuality, and other "non-measurable" qualities, before making their decision about hiring someone.

A good cover letter will do three things:

- Specifically address an employer's needs, based on research.
- Show how your qualifications, skills, and characteristics can address those needs, going well beyond the scope of a resume.
- Ask for a meeting and NOT a job!

In that order!

Why Bother With a Cover Letter – Why Would You Use a Cover Letter – Why is It Important?

If you "are what you write" when it comes to job hunting, particularly at the beginning of a job hunt, then you must maximize your efforts and give an employer more information than what's listed on your resume.

A resume doesn't:

- say why you picked a certain company to contact
- say how, in point by point fashion, you fit the bill for the job they have
- tell your whole story – it tells only the part about jobs, education, and skills
- allow you to address any sensitive areas (like a gap in employment) that, if addressed, could keep you in the running for the job
- say who the recipient of your communication is
- enable your personal style or flair to come through

Therefore, it seems prudent and sensible to take advantage of the power of the cover letter. It's just one more piece of paper for the employer to read, but it's a powerful – and hopefully persuasive – one. It gives you the chance to address what a resume cannot. If the average resume receives less than a minute of an employer's time, sending a good cover letter along with the resume might give you another minute of time when the employer is thinking about you. This one factor alone might increase your time in front of an employer by 200%!

> It's just one more piece of paper for the employer to read, but it's a powerful – and hopefully persuasive – one.

We believe most employers welcome a cover letter, but it must be well-crafted and say something more than just repeating what's already on a resume. Employers are busy, but they are also smart. They want to find the right candidate and they want good information on which to base their decisions to interview or hire. If you make it easy for them to see how you stand apart from other candidates, you will increase your chance to be called in for a meeting, where you can have the time you need to make your case.

There is a school of thought, however, that believes employers don't always welcome a cover letter. This is especially true when it comes to jobs listed on the Internet. An employer can be bombarded with hundreds or thousands of unsolicited resumes, often sent by search firms, which include the canned, "one size fits all" kind of cover letter. Additionally, many job hunters don't take the time to personalize cover letters but instead rely on software programs that generate standard, boring, and useless letters, and this dilutes their impact on, and importance to, employers. Rightfully so, the employer starts to question the authenticity of such letters and doesn't want to waste any time on them.

That's why you **must** take the time to make your cover letter count. Don't write something like this:

> *I read your ad and would like to offer my services to your organization. Enclosed is my resume outlining my work history. I know I am uniquely qualified to do this job. Please call me at your earliest convenience to arrange a meeting. I am most interested in joining your team. Thank you for your time.*

It adds nothing!

Let's turn the tables here and look at this process in a different way. Imagine that as a job hunter you have 200 (or even 50) jobs to choose from and can pick ANY one of them that you want. The catch is that the only information you have about each job is written on one single piece of paper. Without more information, it would be pretty hard to know which might be the best job for you. You would probably want more information and to meet with someone to talk about the job in further detail, see the lay of the land, get a feel for the people you would work with, etc. However, you have to rule out at least 95% of them without the benefit of that extra information. Be pretty tough, don't you think? Well, that's exactly the task placed before many employers. It's hard to make choices when information is limited, but the nature of our job hunting system forces this exact outcome.

That's why a cover letter is your chance to move the odds in your favor. It allows you to add an extra piece or two of information that might make it easier for an employer to invite you in for a meeting.

In the worst-case scenario, let's say you send a letter with your resume to an employer and they prefer to look only at your resume and skip the letter initially. You've lost nothing. They know you took the time to write the letter and if they like what they see on your resume, they may come back to the letter for a minute to actually read what you've written. So, err on the side of sending the letter, even when you think it won't matter! It is better to use every tool you can for the one chance you have with an employer to make your case.

When to Use a Cover Letter

There are three times when different cover letters should be used:

- When responding to a classified ad or job posting in the Open Market; the job hunter has been "invited" to respond.
- When contacting a company without benefit of an "invitation" in the form of an ad or posting; this is an unsolicited approach in the Hidden Market.
- When contacting someone on the referral of a third party, who has suggested you contact a particular company, with his/her recommendation; this is a Referral Letter.

The Invited Response and the Open Market

The job hunter knows there is a job opening and sends a letter in response to an ad. The letter is tailored to the requirements listed in the ad. Refer back to Chapter Three for more information about the Open Market.

The Hidden Market and the Unsolicited Approach

The job hunter has taken the initiative to contact a company that has not advertised a job. The letter is tailored to research conducted on the company after the job hunter has done legwork, homework, and just plain work on finding out about the company, field, job content, and recipient. Refer back to Chapter Five for more information about the Hidden Market.

The Referral Letter

This type of letter has one added feature the other two types of letters don't: it mentions the name of a third person already known, and hopefully respected, by the recipient of the letter. This is the "referral" part. In this letter, the writer will prominently name someone who suggested the contact with the recipient. It's a powerful tool and one that grabs the attention of most employers, at least long enough for them to read the entire letter. Most referral letters come about as the result of networking with other people and are therefore more commonly used in the unsolicited approach. However, it can happen that a job hunter will know someone in a company that has placed an ad, and can benefit from that contact.

The greatest thing about a referral letter is it generally shoots you to the front of the line – if there is a line – with an employer. It can give you a terrific advantage over other candidates by immediately making you a "member of the club," albeit one step removed. You will be afforded more consideration than if you approached the company blindly, without benefit of a recommendation from someone known to both parties, at least in name, if not personally.

What if I Can't Write Well?

Not all of us were born with a Hemingway or Steinbeck in the family tree. Some of us won't take to the written word with ease. It won't be our strong suit and we won't feel comfortable writing letters to employers. We'll think the alternative of paying a resume service a few hundred dollars to churn out a resume and a canned letter will be enough. Then we can send them out and sit back and feel good that we are doing something constructive to find a job.

> The great news about writing a cover letter is that you can take the time to do it right.

That's okay, but when no job offers roll in, you'll need to be ready to start over with a better plan. If you want to get a job or, at the very least, shorten the time it takes to get that job, you will need to send personalized cover letters.

The great news about writing a cover letter is that you can take the time to do it right. You don't have to do it in one hour or in front of others, as you might with other kinds of employment tests. You don't have to do it alone.

The first step is to get some help. There are loads of resources that can help the job hunter learn how to write better. Check out:

- *Woe Is I: The Grammarphobe's Guide to Better English in Plain English*, Second Edition, by Patricia T. O'Conner, (Riverhead Trade, 2004)

- *You Send Me: Getting It Right When You Write Online*, by Patricia T. O'Conner, Stewart Kellerman, (Harcourt, 2002)

- *The Elements of Style,* Fourth Edition, by William Strunk Jr., et al., (Longman, 2000)

- *On Writing Well*, 25th Anniversary Edition, by William Zinsser, (Collins, 2001)

- *Grammatically Correct: The Writer's Essential Guide to Punctuation, Spelling, Style, Usage and Grammar*, by Anne Stilman, (Writer's Digest Books, 1997)

When you have finished your letter, run it by two or three friends who have good writing skills and let them make suggestions and comments about how it might be improved. When you do this, don't lose your own personal voice, but do take to heart helpful suggestions.

Different Styles of Cover Letters

Just as people are different, the style of a cover letter can be different. There are three generally accepted ways to structure a cover letter:

- Traditional Approach
- Mirror Approach
- You-Me-We Approach

Traditional Approach

The first style we call the "traditional" approach to the letter. This is not the authors' favorite style, because the letter is all about the writer, and not the recipient. It's a "Me, Me, Me" letter!

It goes like this:

Opening: The first paragraph is to briefly introduce yourself and say why you are writing to them. You should identify the job you want, so they don't have to guess. In this paragraph, you can include a summary statement of your strengths as a candidate for the particular job.

Body of the Letter: This is your chance to tell the employer about your specific skills, expertise, and experience as they relate to the job. Show them why you are a person they should meet. You can elaborate on why you want the job. Focus on what you can do for them – that's what they care about most.

Closing Paragraph: This final paragraph sets up the plan for follow-up. You will close your letter with an indication of who will be responsible for follow-up, taking responsibility yourself whenever you can. Suggest how and when this contact will take place, either to set up a time for a meeting or to talk in more detail about your qualifications by phone.

This traditional letter will sometimes be four or five paragraphs in length with paragraphs two, three, and four outlining your qualifications. This is especially true when the job is at the mid-manager or higher level and one paragraph won't suffice to tell your story.

Mirror Approach

This style is used when responding to an ad, as it mirrors the qualifications listed in the ad. It is far more graphically effective than the traditional approach. It's a "Me, You, We" letter!

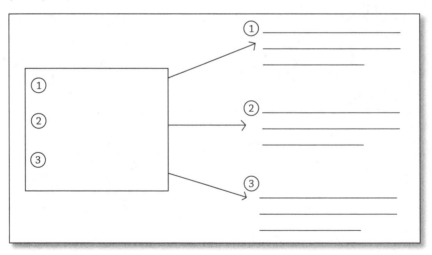

It goes like this:

Opening: You briefly introduce yourself and tell them why you are writing to them. You should reference the ad they placed (Job Title, Location of Ad, Date and Reference #, if one) and give a short summary statement of your strengths as a candidate for the particular job and/or your interest in the job.

Body of Letter: On the left-hand side of the page you list the qualifications they gave in the ad or posting (four or five are enough) and on the right-hand side of the page you show with concrete examples how you meet their qualifications.

Closing Paragraph: This final paragraph establishes the plan for follow-up. You will close your letter with an indication of who will be responsible for follow-up, taking responsibility yourself whenever you can. Suggest how and when this contact will take place, either to arrange a time for a meeting or to talk in more detail about your qualifications by phone.

This letter does not follow a traditional paragraph form. Graphically, the qualifications or requirements listed in the ad need to face the examples you list from your background, so they will stand out and the employer will immediately see your strengths.

The You-Me-We Approach

This style is the favorite of the authors as it addresses the recipient's interest and needs first, then the job applicant's interest and qualifications, and then the hopeful marriage of the two as employer/employee. It is commonly used for an unsolicited approach. Finally, the right order, "You-Me-We" letter!

It goes like this:

Opening: YOU (meaning the employer)

Contrary to what most people have been taught, it's paramount that the opening of your letter speak to the reader's needs. To be effective, the reader must come first! The first sentence should create surprise and intrigue and show your reader that you have considered what is important to them. Show them that you care enough to want to respond to their ad or have selected them because what they do really appeals to you and you have done some research on their company/field/industry. If you don't make them feel they are special to you, you won't be special to them. After you have opened with a sentence about the company/field/industry and gotten their attention, you can add a sentence or two about your interest in the particular job, taking care to name the job specifically and state what you offer.

Body of the Letter: ME (meaning the job hunter)

In this paragraph, tell the employer about your specific skills, expertise, and experience as they relate to the job. Show them why you are a person they should want to meet. You can elaborate on why you want the job. Focus on what you can do for them. Illustrate what you say with quantifiable achievements or tasks that have tangible results.

Closing Paragraph: WE (meaning the two together)

If you've done a good job with your first paragraphs, hopefully you will have convinced the employer to meet with you. This paragraph sets the plan of action for follow-up to the letter.

This style of letter departs from traditional advice and therefore might be a bit scarier for the job hunter to contemplate using. In order for this to be effective, you have to do some research on the company/industry that is meaningful and will catch their attention.

What Do All these Letters Have in Common?

No matter what style of letter you use, there are several things they all have in common:

- Every letter sent to an employer should consider **their** needs, and not yours as the job hunter.
- Every letter sent should be addressed to a **specific** person. If you don't send your letter to a real person identified by name, your chance for success is reduced drastically.

- Every letter sent should be **error-free**. Don't allow a letter to go out without checking and double-checking for mistakes.
- Every letter sent should be **customized** to the job being sought and the employer being contacted. It's not sufficient to write a one-size-fits-all. Don't use a canned approach. Be creative. Be original. Be honest.

When you've done a good job, your cover letter will have:

- Served as a vehicle to introduce you to an employer.
- Demonstrated to the employer you know something about them, their company, their industry, and the job you want.
- Related your experience directly to the employer's needs.
- Explained to the employer why you chose to contact them and what position you are seeking.
- Told the employer something about who you are and what you can do and have done.
- Provided a more detailed account of your skills and experience than your resume – it expands on the resume with relevant information that wasn't included on it, usually due to length constraints; it will act as a magnifying glass of sorts – allowing you to zero in on the really relevant information.
- Directed them to relevant points of interest clearly and concisely.
- Shown your genuine interest in them.
- Allowed your style and personality to show through so they can see how you express yourself.
- Proven you are a person who goes the extra mile to tailor your correspondence to them and them alone.
- Enticed them to want to learn more about you!

It's Time to Write Your Letter

By now, we hope you understand and can embrace the importance of writing a good cover letter. You should understand the importance of making your letter stand out, doing the needed research to target your job search, and knowing when and how to deal with sensitive issues, and what style of letter to use.

Remember, you are writing a business letter. That means your letter must be concise, brief, and grab the reader's interest. This letter is not meant to tell your whole story, only enough to make your reader want to know more.

It is imperative that you follow standard business practices when writing your letter. This is not the time to experiment with zany styles to show how creative you can be, nor the time to try out your poetry skills, or show that you can include every detail from your work life – no novellas here! This is not the time to experiment with funky type styles or irregular paper.

We are talking about one page (at most, two). Your letter will be judged on the small things, as well as its content. If you don't use the right format, correct grammar and punctuation, it will be noticed. If you letter adds nothing more than what your resume already says, it will be noticed. If you don't suggest any plan for follow-up, it will be noticed. If you make even one typographical error, it will be noticed.

There are basically only two accepted styles of business letters. One is called "**Full Block,**" where all elements of the letter are aligned to the left margin. The other is called "**Modified Block,**" where the sender's address, date, complimentary closing, signature, and typed name are aligned down the middle of the page. All other elements of the letters are aligned to the left. Either style is fine for your letter.

There are enough other factors at work in this whole job hunting process that rule people "in" or "out." Don't add fuel to an already brightly burning fire. If you are to be ruled out, let it be because someone else was better qualified than you for the job, not because you didn't present yourself well in a letter and/or a resume.

It's like running a race. We can all appreciate, or at least begrudgingly understand, when someone runs faster than we do to win the race. What's harder to live with is knowing you tripped yourself up when you didn't need to. You probably wouldn't start the race with one shoe untied. You would know that there would be a pretty good chance you would fall. Same here. Don't trip yourself up unnecessarily. Tie your shoes!

It's time to get started with a step-by-step approach to writing your letter.

2 Section Two
Building Your
Letter Step By Step

Chapter **9**

Step 1: The Sender's Information

Location in the Letter

The sender's information is located in the left top corner of the letter, when using a Full Block style. When using a Modified Block style, this element will be centered. If using pre-printed letterhead, the name and address of the sender are usually printed across the top section of the paper, although some variations exist on this.

Full Block

John Smith
6 Hope Street
Anytown, CA 55555
555-123-4567

January 1, 20XX

Ms. Sue Jones
Production Manager
ABC Company
1234 First Street
Anytown, CA 55555

Dear Ms. Jones:

Your company has developed a unique safety device for wheelchairs that has only been copied by two competitors up to this time. I have thought of two additional ways to improve these wheelchairs that will make copying these safety devices very difficult.

I completed my studies as a mechanical technician at the ABC College last fall and have always been involved with concerns dealing with people who have physical limitations. I am currently active in a non-profit organization, which concentrates on access availability for wheelchairs in high-rise buildings in Anytown.

I have already had the opportunity to work on two projects while in college:

- Marketing: developed 17 technical brochures for a packaging company with $15 million in sales per year;
- Productivity: improved an assembly line for high tech products, resulting in a 17% growth in efficiency in one year.

I would welcome a call from you to set up a meeting. I can be reached at 555-123-4567.

Sincerely,

John Smith

Pre-printed Letterhead Location or Modified Block

John Smith
6 Hope Street
Anytown, CA 55555
555-123-4567

January 1, 20XX

Ms. Sue Jones
Production Manager
ABC Company
1234 First Street
Anytown, CA 55555

Dear Ms. Jones:

Your company has developed a unique safety device for wheelchairs that has only been copied by two competitors up to this time. I have thought of two additional ways to improve these wheelchairs that will make copying these safety devices very difficult.

I completed my studies as a mechanical technician at the ABC College last fall and have always been involved with concerns dealing with people who have physical limitations. I am currently active in a non-profit organization, which concentrates on access availability for wheelchairs in high-rise buildings in Anytown.

I have already had the opportunity to work on two projects while in college:

- Marketing: developed 17 technical brochures for a packaging company with $15 million in sales per year;
- Productivity: improved an assembly line for high tech products, resulting in a 17% growth in efficiency in one year.

I would welcome a call from you to set up a meeting. I can be reached at 555-123-4567.

Sincerely,

John Smith

Reason and Purpose

Placing your name and address at the top of the letter allows the reader to immediately see who is sending the letter. It will subtly reassure the reader, in an almost unconscious way, that someone who is confident enough to place their name at the beginning of the document has written the letter. It lends a professional look to the letter and provides a way for the reader to return correspondence if they desire.

Degree of Difficulty

This item is very easy for most of us. It consists of name, address, and city/state/zip – country, if international. Most letterheads will also have a phone number and an email address or fax number. If you're using pre-printed letterhead, you will not need to spend time on this item.

The only questions that might arise if not using letterhead are whether you will list a title for yourself and/or include phone numbers – landline, cell phone, fax or message numbers – and/or an email address.

Importance in the Letter

It is very important to include your contact information in the letter. Not only does a letter without it look unprofessional, it does not allow an employer to contact you easily if they are interested in your candidacy. Be sure to put this as your first item when composing your letter.

Specifics

This is a short item and should be no longer than five or six lines, at most. It should be left flush to the margin or centered, at the top of the letter. It should include:

- Your first name, middle initial (if you normally use one), and last name
- Your full street address, including apartment number
- City, state, and zip code
- Your country, for international letters only

Other optional information you may list:

- Your landline phone number
- Your cell or mobile phone number
- A message number, in lieu of another phone number.
- Your email address
- Your fax number
- A title or degree, if appropriate, such as Dr. or Ph.D.

You should not list all of the above. If you list more than one phone number, use only one line for all of them, otherwise this will take up valuable space on your page that could better be used for conveying your qualifications to the employer.

Do This . . .

It is sufficient to note only your name and address if you wish. You can place telephone and email information in the last paragraph of your letter.

If you list a title or degree, limit it to a single one. If you choose to do this, consider whether this will alienate the reader by making you sound pompous, or create some kind of mutual bond if you are members of the same club or graduates of the same university. This will require you know some facts about the recipient of the letter.

If you choose to list your landline phone number, remember that you will not always be home to take your calls. Make sure that your recorded greeting is professional. While it is cute to have your children singing the theme to SpongeBob SquarePants, it doesn't lend itself to the professional impression you want to create. You also run the risk of someone answering the phone in your absence who does not know how to take a proper message, or loses it and never passes it on to you.

If you choose to list a message number and don't have a line dedicated to your job hunting activities, ask someone to help you who can take your calls during regular office hours and is comfortable and professional sounding on the phone. Go over with them how they should handle the calls that might come in and what information they should get from the employer, so you can get back in touch with them. Brief them on how to limit their responses so they are not subjected to an inquisition about you, which, if handled poorly, could screen you out.

Don't Do This . . .

- Omit the sender's name.
- Write the word "Title" or "Degree" in the sender's information.
- List all your academic degrees or titles.
- Attach a photograph of yourself.
- List too many telephone numbers or email addresses.

If you choose to list your cell phone number, remember that you might be called at times that are not convenient for you to take the call in a professional manner. If you are at the ballpark eating hotdogs and drinking beer or trying to get your child to stop crying in the car, you won't be ready to take the call. You run the risk of being caught off guard and unprepared, and your first person-to-person contact with the employer will suffer.

Examples of Mistakes to Avoid in the Sender's Information

Listing Too Many Titles:

Mr. John Smith
Graduate of ABC University
International Expert in Value Analysis
President of the ABC Chapter of CDF Group
6 Hope Street
Anytown, CA 55555

Listing Too Many Telephone Numbers or Email Addresses:

Ms. Sally Smith
6 Hope Street
Anytown, CA 55555
555-123-4567 Home
555-234-5678 Cell
555-345-6789 Message
555-456-7890 Fax
sallysmith@sallysmith.com
sallygirl@abc.com
SSnumber1@cdf.com

Not Including Sender's Name:

6 Hope Street
Anytown, CA 55555

Using the Word "Title":

Mr. Joe Jones
Title: Department Manager
6 Hope Street
Anytown, CA 55555
555-123-4567

Examples of How to Set Up the Sender's Information

Sally Smith
Graduate of ABC University
6 Hope Street
Anytown, CA 55555

Mr. John Smith
6 Hope Street
Anytown, CA 55555
555-123-4567
johnsmith@johnsmith.com

Ms. Sally Smith
Certified Public Accountant
6 Hope Street
Anytown, CA 55555
555-123-4567
Sallysmith@sallysmith.com

Chapter 10

Step 2: The Date

Location in the Letter

The date should be located directly below the sender's information, leaving one or two spaces between lines. If using Full Block style, it will be aligned to the left margin. If using Modified Block style or letterhead, it will be aligned under the sender's address in the middle of the page.

Full Block

John Smith
6 Hope Street
Anytown, CA 55555
555-123-4567

January 1, 20XX

Ms. Sue Jones
Production Manager
ABC Company
1234 First Street
Anytown, CA 55555

Dear Ms. Jones:

Your company has developed a unique safety device for wheelchairs that has only been copied by two competitors up to this time. I have thought of two additional ways to improve these wheelchairs that will make copying these safety devices very difficult.

I completed my studies as a mechanical technician at the ABC College last fall and have always been involved with concerns dealing with people who have physical limitations. I am currently active in a non-profit organization, which concentrates on access availability for wheelchairs in high-rise buildings in Anytown.

I have already had the opportunity to work on two projects while in college:

- Marketing: developed 17 technical brochures for a packaging company with $15 million in sales per year;
- Productivity: improved an assembly line for high tech products, resulting in a 17% growth in efficiency in one year.

I would welcome a call from you to set up a meeting. I can be reached at 555-123-4567.

Sincerely,

John Smith

Modified Block or Letterhead

John Smith
6 Hope Street
Anytown, CA 55555
555-123-4567

January 1, 20XX

Ms. Sue Jones
Production Manager
ABC Company
1234 First Street
Anytown, CA 55555

Dear Ms. Jones:

Your company has developed a unique safety device for wheelchairs that has only been copied by two competitors up to this time. I have thought of two additional ways to improve these wheelchairs that will make copying these safety devices very difficult.

I completed my studies as a mechanical technician at the ABC College last fall and have always been involved with concerns dealing with people who have physical limitations. I am currently active in a non-profit organization, which concentrates on access availability for wheelchairs in high-rise buildings in Anytown.

I have already had the opportunity to work on two projects while in college:

- Marketing: developed 17 technical brochures for a packaging company with $15 million in sales per year;
- Productivity: improved an assembly line for high tech products, resulting in a 17% growth in efficiency in one year.

I would welcome a call from you to set up a meeting. I can be reached at 555-123-4567.

Sincerely,

John Smith

Reason and Purpose

Every letter should have the date on it to look professional. This allows the sender to remember when the letter was written and gauge if the time for follow-up is at hand. It allows the recipient to know when you first contacted them and how much time has elapsed between the receipt of your letter and their response to you.

Degree of Difficulty

This item presents no difficulty. A look at the calendar will provide the correct date!

Importance in the Letter

The date is a must. Sending a letter without it lacks professionalism and could cause confusion on the part of the reader. Without a date, the reader won't know if your letter was written yesterday or a year ago, which means it will be thrown away.

Specifics

It will fit on one line and should contain nothing but month, day, and year. Some people like to put the name of the day as well.

Do This . . .

- You may add the name of the day if you want. For example: *Monday, January 1, 2006*.

- Write out the entire name of the month and do not use figures. For example, use "January" and not "1" or "01." This will avoid errors and ambiguity.

- Spell the name of the month correctly.

- Follow the custom used in the country to which you are writing. For example, in some continental European countries it is common practice to place the day first, then the month, then the year. For example: *4-February-2005*.

Don't Do This . . .

- Use a numeric form, which will be misunderstood, in countries where the day and month are inverted.

- Make any spelling mistakes.

- Use abbreviations.

- Leave out commas between day and year.

Examples of Mistakes to Avoid With the Date

Listing Date of Ad and Not Current Date:

Tuesday, Date of Ad November 1, 2006

Using Just Numbers for the Date:

12/08/06

Making Typographical Mistakes:

March 34, 2006

Deceber 8th, 2006

January 4 2006

Examples of How to Write the Date

Friday, February 25, 2006

February 25th, 2006

February 25, 2006

25, February, 2006 (International)

Chapter 11

Step 3: The Recipient

Location in the Letter

The recipient's name, title (or department if known), company name, and address should come below the date. Leave one line between the recipient's data and the date line. Align to the left margin.

John Smith
6 Hope Street
Anytown, CA 55555
555-123-4567

January 1, 20XX

Ms. Sue Jones
Production Manager
ABC Company
1234 First Street
Anytown, CA 55555

Dear Ms. Jones:

Your company has developed a unique safety device for wheelchairs that has only been copied by two competitors up to this time. I have thought of two additional ways to improve these wheelchairs that will make copying these safety devices very difficult.

I completed my studies as a mechanical technician at the ABC College last fall and have always been involved with concerns dealing with people who have physical limitations. I am currently active in a non-profit organization, which concentrates on access availability for wheelchairs in high-rise buildings in Anytown.

I have already had the opportunity to work on two projects while in college:

- Marketing: developed 17 technical brochures for a packaging company with $15 million in sales per year;
- Productivity: improved an assembly line for high tech products, resulting in a 17% growth in efficiency in one year.

I would welcome a call from you to set up a meeting. I can be reached at 555-123-4567.

Sincerely,

John Smith

Reason and Purpose

Every letter needs a place to go! Without the name and address of the recipient, your letter doesn't have much chance to get to the correct person and you will ultimately not reach your objective. You can spend your time and energy writing the best letter in the world, but if it doesn't get to the person who is interested in what you are offering and has the power to call you in for a meeting, your chances for success are diminished.

It is paramount for success that you start any letter-writing effort by getting the name of the person to whom you will send your letter. This will require you to do some research when you do not know the name of the person to whom you want to send your letter. If you know the name of this person, you are ahead of the game and can proceed with relative ease on this item.

If you send your letter to the wrong person or, worse yet, to the following, don't expect much. You have lost your chance to make a good first impression, and in most cases your letter will be thrown out without consideration.

- "the person responsible of the after-sales service"
- "the person in charge of Human Resources"
- the company or organization without any indication of a recipient's name and/or department and/or division
- "to whom it may concern"

Degree of Difficulty

This can be the hardest part of the letter to get right if you don't know who to contact. With practice, most people can find ways to talk about their skills and interest in a particular job in a convincing manner. What can't be done is to "make up" this part of the letter. You can't pull a name out of the air. You **have** to get this part right. An error here proves fatal in most instances.

Not only is it imperative that you have the name of a recipient, but the **correct** recipient. The correct recipient is the person who will be able to appreciate what you have to offer - maybe not H.R. - and, in many cases, the one who will make the decision about meeting you and/or hiring you. This person may also end up being your boss if you are hired. At the very least, this person may redirect your letter to the proper person, if it turns out they are not the one to make the final decision.

Importance in the Letter

As stated before, this is the most important aspect of the letter. Your ability to send your letter to the right person and to get their name, title, and address correct will account for at least 50% of the success of your approach. You cannot afford to be wrong on this element. Even if you have the most incredible offer and fabulous design, if you are wrong here, you lose.

Many companies now, as policy, will not even bother to read letters and resumes that are not directed to a specific person in the organization. They believe - rightfully so - that when the writer of the letter cannot be bothered to find out the name of the person they want to reach, they need not be bothered with reading the letter. In these organizations, knowing the correct recipient accounts for 100% of your success, at least initially!

Specialists in the area of mass mailings will confirm that, of the three essential parameters to any mailing,

- the **recipient** accounts for 50% the success of your mailing
- the **offer/proposal** accounts for 35% the success of your mailing
- the **look/appearance** accounts for 15% the success of your mailing

When we learn from the professionals in the mailing business, we understand that the person who is to get the letter becomes even more important than what is said or how the letter looks – and we should weigh our efforts accordingly.

Specifics

This is a short item and should be no longer than five or six lines, at most. It should be left flush to the margin, below the date line. It should include:

- the full name of the recipient, including social title - Mr., Mrs., Miss, Ms., Dr., The Rev'd, etc., if known
- their title, if known
- the company name
- their department or division, if needed
- the company address – full street address, including suite or floor numbers
- city, state, and zip code
- country (if international) and/or country code

If you have two names and are unsure which person to send your letter, select the higher-ranking person in the organization. It is easier to move a letter down a level in most organizations than it is to move up! It's much more likely that a Vice President would send a letter down to a Department Manager, than the other way around.

Do This . . .

Be sure you have the **correct name** of the person you wish to contact. Verify the spelling of the name. Find out the gender of the person you are contacting so you do not make a mistake with the social title.

Be sure you have the **correct title** for the person you are addressing. If the person has an honorary title, use it. If you have to guess whether to use a title, err on the side of including it, as some people are offended if you leave out their title.

Be sure you have the **complete and correct address**. Even if you think you have done your homework and have the correct name, title, and address, verify it using at least two sources. You can use the phone book (if it's local), the company's Internet site, a classified ad, or printed information such as a brochure or annual report. Best of all, you should call the company before sending the letter to verify it. That way there will be no mistakes. Make it your practice to double-check everything – using at least two different sources.

If you know the name of the person you wish to contact, simply call the company and tell the person who answers the phone that you are sending a letter to Mr. Smith and want to verify the spelling of his name. Even Smith could be spelled Smyth or Smithe – don't assume anything! Check the title and the correct address. You can read the information you have, if you wish, and let them correct you if there is a mistake. This will legitimize your query.

If you do not know the name, title, address, or gender of the person you wish to reach, you should call the company and ask for the name of the person in charge of _____. You will have to know the general area, at least.

When you are supplied a name, you can then ask for the exact spelling of their name (first and last – this can sometimes help you determine gender – but not always!), their exact title, and the address. For example:

> "Hello. My name is Peter Smith. I am sending a letter, which is confidential but not urgent, to the person in charge of the after-sales service. Could you please tell me the exact spelling of their name? Of his/her first name? His/her exact title? Thank you very much for your help."

If you telephone a company and the call goes to an automated voice mail introduction system, listen carefully to your choices. You might be able to learn the name of the person you want to contact from the list. If you are not given choices, but told you can enter the number of any extension at any time, you will have to select the option that connects you to a real person. Sometimes if the company's telephone number ends in 00, you can try pushing 01, or 02, and see if you will be connected to someone. It might be that the following lines/extensions are given numerically to people, in order of their importance – i.e., President – 01, V.P. – 02. Pushing an extension might allow you to bypass the automatic call answering system.

If you cannot get the name of the person by calling the company, for whatever reason, more research in business directories or on the Internet may be needed. Keep trying all possible sources of information. If you can find the name of even one person, you can use it to help you arrive at the right person. For example:

> *Hello. My name is Peter Smith. I am sending a letter to the person in charge of after-sales and want to verify I have the right person. I believe it is Mr. Jones. Oh, that isn't the correct person? Can you tell me the name of that person, so my letter gets to him/her? Thank you. Just to be sure, can you verify the spelling of the last name? First name? And their title? Thank you very much.*

If all this fails and if you feel bold, you can call the company and ask to be connected to the person in charge of "Accounts Receivable" – usually in the accounting department. This person is likely to know most of the people in the company and is rarely contacted by a friendly person, instead getting calls mostly from disgruntled people over money issues. You can ask them for the name of the person in charge of _____, and see if they will supply it. They may ask how you were connected with them, and you can say you asked to speak with someone knowledgeable about the company.

If you feel that you would be too nervous to do this yourself, seek the help of a friend who is good on the phone and has nothing invested emotionally. They will not be nervous and will stand a better chance to get the information.

If you have absolutely no idea whom to contact, you will have to guess:

- In a small or average size company (5 to 25 people), choose to send your letter to the "Number 1" person, hoping it will work its way down to the appropriate person.

- In a large organization (over 100 people), choose the Vice President of the area that interests you, or, better yet, the assistant of the Vice President.

- In a multinational organization (thousands of employees), choose the Department Head of the division that interests you and is geographically suitable for you.

Don't Do This . . .

- Use a title for someone that is below their actual rank. If you have to guess, it is better to promote the person! You will be forgiven for that.
- Misspell the name, title, or address.
- Use the wrong social title – Mr., Mrs., Ms., Dr., etc.
- Write to the "General Manager of the ABC Company." This is too vague and will have the same result as if you had addressed your letter to "To Whom It May Concern."
- Send it to the wrong department or division – your letter will be thrown away in 99.9% of cases. It is not their job to track down the right office for you!

Examples of Mistakes to Avoid for the Recipient

Being Too Informal:

Susan
ABC Company
1234 First Street
Anytown, CA 55555

Not Naming a Specific Person as Recipient:

To Whom it May Concern
ABC Company
1234 First Street
Anytown, CA 55555

To the Person In Charge of Recruitment
ABC Company
1234 First Street
Anytown, CA 55555

To the Personnel Manager
ABC Company
1234 First Street
Anytown, CA 55555

H.R. Manager
ABC Company
1234 First Street
Anytown, CA 55555

Making Spelling or Typographical Errors:

Mr. Susan Smithe
Assitant to the President
ABC Company
1600 Floor
1234 First Street
Anytown, CA 55555

Using an Inappropriate Title:

Joe Black
Main Security Guy
ABC Company
1234 First Street
Anytown, CA 55555

Examples Recommended for the Recipient

Mr. Peter Smith
In Charge of After Sales Service
ABC Company
1234 First Street
Anytown, CA 55555

Ms. Jane Jones
President of the Board
ABC Company
1234 First Street
Anytown, CA 55555

Mrs. Susan Smith
Marketing Associate
Public Relations Department
ABC Company
1234 First Street, Suite 11
Anytown, CA 55555

Mr. Joe Jones
ABC Company
1234 First Street
Anytown, CA 55555

Chapter 12

Step 4: The Reference Line

Location in the Letter

The reference or subject line is located between the recipient's information and the salutation. There is one line space between it and each of those two items. Align to the left margin.

```
John Smith
6 Hope Street
Anytown, CA  55555
555-123-4567


January 1, 20XX


Ms. Sue Jones
Production Manager
ABC Company
1234 First Street
Anytown, CA  55555


Subject: New Technology in Wheelchair Development

Dear Ms. Jones:


Your company has developed a unique safety device for wheelchairs that has only been copied by two
competitors up to this time. I have thought of two additional ways to improve these wheelchairs that
will make copying these safety devices very difficult.

I completed my studies as a mechanical technician at the ABC College last fall and have always been
involved with concerns dealing with people who have physical limitations.  I am currently active
in a non-profit organization, which concentrates on access availability for wheelchairs in high-rise
buildings in Anytown.

I have already had the opportunity to work on two projects while in college:

   ■  Marketing: developed 17 technical brochures for a packaging company with $15 million in sales
       per year;
   ■  Productivity:  improved an assembly line for high tech products, resulting in a 17% growth in
       efficiency in one year.

I would welcome a call from you to set up a meeting.  I can be reached at 555-123-4567.

Sincerely,


John Smith
```

Reason and Purpose

The purpose of this item is to quickly define the subject and reason for your letter. It should tell the reader, within two seconds, why you have written to them.

- **Ad:** If you are responding to an ad it allows you to note:
  - the title of the position to be filled
  - the name of the media where ad was posted (newspaper, magazine, trade journal, Internet site)
  - the date of the ad
  - the reference number of the ad, if any

- **UL (Unsolicited Letter):** If you are writing an unsolicited letter, the purpose of this item is to grab the attention of the reader and make them want to read your entire letter. It is a teaser of sorts, to pique the interest of the reader.

Degree of Difficulty

- **Ad:** This item carries only a small degree of difficulty, particularly when you are responding to an ad. You list the above information to let the reader know which job you are interested in, and move on to the next item. Be sure to list information correctly.

- **UL:** In the case of an unsolicited approach, your reference line will take more thought to ensure it is interesting and appropriate. You will need to carefully think out what to write here.

In no case do you want to use this line to say, "Job-hunting" or "Position Desired." Do not place yourself in the role of a "Job-Beggar." Always proceed as a "Resource Person."

Importance in the Letter

This item is important, as it immediately references the reason for your letter, but it is not essential. In most cases, your letter will not automatically be discarded if this item is missing.

- **Ad:** When responding to an ad, this item should always be filled in so the reader knows immediately which job your letter references, as they may have advertised more than one job – don't make them guess. Since you will have all the information from the ad, this will be easy to complete.

It will also allow you to save space in the opening, body, and closing of your letter for more important information.

- **UL:** You can chose to bypass this item if you are unsure what to say, particularly in the case of the unsolicited approach. It is better to leave this blank than to use a generic – and therefore meaningless – reference, like "Job Wanted" or "I am the candidate for you." If you are not certain that the impact of your reference line will be positive to the reader, you may choose to skip it and move directly into the body of the letter.

Specifics

The reference line, in most cases, is one line only in length. In some cases, it may be two lines. Do not exceed this length.

It is concise in its nature, so you may use fragments here rather than complete sentences when appropriate. If using a fragment, you do not need ending punctuation. If using a complete sentence, use a period at the end. Questions and exclamations are better used elsewhere!

It is usually written as:

- RE:
- Reference:
- REFERENCE:
- SUBJECT:
- Object:

You may also use (although not as common):

- Item:
- Concern:
- Topic:

If you plan to make a "SPECIAL DELIVERY," "PERSONAL," or "CONFIDENTIAL" notation, you will move down one line and type it here. Do not place these notations on the reference line. These notations are rarely used anymore, so consider if they are important enough to include on your letter.

Do This . . .

- Be concise without being too specific.
- Adopt a "low profile" approach, rather than trying to be too bold.
- Say something here that grabs your reader's interest and pertains to their needs and not your own.
- **Ad:** If responding to an ad, use this line to reference the job title, publication name, date of the ad, and reference number (if one is listed). You may use the line to highlight something about yourself that relates to the job and arouses the reader's interest. In this case, the first paragraph of your letter must reference the ad to which you are responding.
- **UL:** Describe a very specific advantage you have to offer.

Don't Do This . . .

- Write a reference that is vague and unclear and causes confusion for your reader.
- Use jargon or slang.
- Write too much – do not use long sentences.
- Say, "query for information" or "request for a meeting."
- Use a topic that is so generic it is meaningless.
- List an objective that meets your needs, and not the reader's.
- Use this line to say "Personal" or "Confidential."
- Use this line to say "Special Delivery."
- **UL:** In the case of an unsolicited approach, do not
    - mention job-hunting or application in this line.
    - write something that doesn't inspire you – surely it won't inspire the reader either!
    - tell them what is wrong with their company and how you can fix it.

Examples of Mistakes to Avoid in Your Reference Line

Ad

Stating Anything About Wanting a Job:

> **Object:** *Job Application*
> **Re:** *Request for Meeting*
> **Object:** *Application*

Boasting About Yourself:

> **Reference:** *I am the answer to your problems*

Not Providing Full Reference for Ad:

> **Subject:** *Your advertisement in the L.A. Times*
> **Subject:** *Your ad in the press*

UL

Stating Anything About Wanting a Job:

> **Re:** *Application*
> **Subject:** *Job hunting*

Telling Them What is Wrong With Their Company:

> **Object:** *Improvement of your efficiency*
> **Reference:** *Optimization of your underdeveloped production*

Boasting About Yourself:

> **Reference:** *I can make your company profitable*

Being too Wordy and Unspecific:

> **Reference:** *I am aware that your company is on the forefront of technology and is at the top of the list in your industry. I am very well qualified to join your team, proved by my 15 years of experience at various high-tech firms in the Valley, and a desire to be part of a forward-thinking company.*

Examples of Language Recommended for Your Reference Line

Ad

Subject: Your ad for an Administrative Assistant, published in the L.A. Times, on May 17th, 2005, under the reference number 123456

Reference: Fourteen Years of Administrative Experience Qualifies Me for Your Administrative Assistant Position, Ad # 123456

UL

Object: 3 New Sources of Copper Energy Supply Found

Reference: Decrease of more than 60% of thefts in a supermarket

Ref: Increase of Customer Loyalty by 52%

RE: Teaching Software Literacy in 40% Less Time

Reference: Simple Method to Avoid Stock Overages

Subject: Technique to Increase Customer Loyalty

Concern: 16% Reduction in Breakdowns of Data Networks

Subject: 60% Reduction of Waste

Topic: Decrease of Reporting Time from 5 Days to 2 Days

Item: Following Up With Delinquent Customers

Chapter **13**
Step 5: The Salutation

Location in the Letter

The salutation is found after the reference line and right above the opening paragraph of your letter. Align to the left margin. If there is no reference line, it will follow the date.

John Smith
6 Hope Street
Anytown, CA 55555
555-123-4567

January 1, 20XX

Ms. Sue Jones
Production Manager
ABC Company
1234 First Street
Anytown, CA 55555

Dear Ms. Jones:

Your company has developed a unique safety device for wheelchairs that has only been copied by two competitors up to this time. I have thought of two additional ways to improve these wheelchairs that will make copying these safety devices very difficult.

I completed my studies as a mechanical technician at the ABC College last fall and have always been involved with concerns dealing with people who have physical limitations. I am currently active in a non-profit organization, which concentrates on access availability for wheelchairs in high-rise buildings in Anytown.

I have already had the opportunity to work on two projects while in college:

- Marketing: developed 17 technical brochures for a packaging company with $15 million in sales per year;
- Productivity: improved an assembly line for high tech products, resulting in a 17% growth in efficiency in one year.

I would welcome a call from you to set up a meeting. I can be reached at 555-123-4567.

Sincerely,

John Smith

Reason and Purpose

This item is purely conventional and corresponds to accepted business letter practice. It is a form of politeness in addressing the recipient of the letter. It is a way to say "Hello" and begin your letter.

Degree of Difficulty

The difficulty of this item is relatively minor once you know the name of the recipient of your letter. You must apply the rules of propriety only – conformity to the standards of politeness that are conventionally accepted by society. The only difficulties are making sure that you spell the person's name correctly and use the proper social title (Mr., Mrs., Ms., Dr.) before the name.

Importance in the Letter

This item may not be skipped, as it is a matter of basic politeness and the way to move into the body of your letter.

Specifics

It is one line only, consisting of the word "Dear" or "Hello," a person's social title (Mr., Mrs., Ms., etc.) and the person's name, followed by a colon for punctuation. Use the person's full name to show respect if you do not know them. If you are familiar with the person to whom you are writing and they have asked you to use their first name, you may do so here, but only if it would seem false to go back to their more formal name. Do not guess at the spelling of their name or their gender.

Do This . . .

- Know exactly whom you want to contact.
- Know their title.
- Know their gender.
- Spell social titles and names correctly; never leave this to chance.
- Observe standard business etiquette for the country of your recipient (a different style may be the norm in countries other than the U.S.).
- Show respect for the person you are contacting by using their proper name and the proper social title and do not assume an informality you have not yet earned.
- Use plural forms of social titles if your letter is going to more than one person.

- Mr. – Messrs.
- Mrs. – Mesdames
- Miss – Misses
- Ms. – Mses. or Mss.

Don't Do This . . .

- Make a spelling mistake in their name.
- Guess at their gender and use the wrong social title.
- Ignore their gender (find out if the person is male or female).
- Use their first name if you do not know them well and have not been asked to call them by their first name.
- Use "Your Honor" or other title without knowing its validity and correct form.
- Write to "Whom It May Concern." It will concern no one when this is the case.
- Write to "Dear Madam" or "Dear Sir."
- If writing to a woman, do not use Miss or Mrs., unless you are sure of their marital status and know that they prefer Miss or Mrs. to Ms. It is better to use Ms. in all cases when you are unsure.

Examples of Mistakes to Avoid in Your Salutation

Using Over-Sophisticated Language:

Mister General President Manager:
Madam Manageress of Sales:

Being Too Familiar:

Dear Billy:
Dear Polly:

Being Too Impersonal:

Madam or Sir:
Sirs:
To whom it may concern:
To the department head:
To the person in charge of _____:

Using a Only a Social Title or Other Title:

> Dear Reverend:
> Dear Head of Surgery:
> Dear Miss:
> Dear Person in charge of After-Sales:

Examples of Formats Recommended for Your Salutation

Dear Ms. Smith:
Dear Mr. Jones:
Dear Miss Little:
Hello Paul:
Ms. President:
Dear General Secretary White:
Dear Dr. Black:
Dear Messrs. Smith and Jones:

Chapter 14

Step 6: The Opening Paragraph

Location in the Letter

The first paragraph of your letter is your opening. It follows directly below the salutation. Align to the left margin.

John Smith
6 Hope Street
Anytown, CA 55555
555-123-4567

January 1, 20XX

Ms. Sue Jones
Production Manager
ABC Company
1234 First Street
Anytown, CA 55555

Dear Ms. Jones:

Your company has developed a unique safety device for wheelchairs that has only been copied by two competitors up to this time. I have thought of two additional ways to improve these wheelchairs that will make copying these safety devices very difficult.

I completed my studies as a mechanical technician at the ABC College last fall and have always been involved with concerns dealing with people who have physical limitations. I am currently active in a non-profit organization, which concentrates on access availability for wheelchairs in high-rise buildings in Anytown.

I have already had the opportunity to work on two projects while in college:

- Marketing: developed 17 technical brochures for a packaging company with $15 million in sales per year;
- Productivity: improved an assembly line for high tech products, resulting in a 17% growth in efficiency in one year.

I would welcome a call from you to set up a meeting. I can be reached at 555-123-4567.

Sincerely,

John Smith

Reason and Purpose

The opening paragraph of your letter is of critical importance and must be handled properly. If your opening paragraph is good and grabs the reader's interest, your entire letter will likely be read and considered. If you handle it poorly, however, your letter may be discarded swiftly and you will not get the result you wanted.

Experience tells us that most people don't get this paragraph right – they mistakenly believe this entire paragraph should be devoted to talking about themselves and not the addressing the interests of the person/company to whom they are writing. Contrary to what most people have been taught, it's paramount that the opening of your letter speak to the reader's needs. So, the first line should create surprise and intrigue and show your reader that you value them. Show them that you have done some research on their company/field/industry and care enough to want to respond to their ad or have selected them to contact because what they do really appeals to you. If you don't make them feel they are special to you, you won't be special to them (and the letter will hit the trash can!) Make that first paragraph shout, *"Hey, read this letter! It's worth your time!"*

Don't make this paragraph too long; it is an introduction to the rest of your letter and should set the stage for the body of the letter.

Degree of Difficulty

Many people feel this is one of the most difficult sections to write. Knowing where to start isn't always easy. It's like a race; getting out of the blocks when the gun sounds is the hardest part. Once you are moving, you pick up speed and continue to the finish line with relative ease. But you have to get out of the blocks fast and efficiently. Same with your letter.

Doing some research on the company/field/industry can alleviate this difficulty. Find a few interesting facts that might make a good opening line for your letter. Pick facts that particularly interest you or relate to your background and skills. Write several different examples and see which one feels most meaningful and natural to you, and use that as your first sentence.

Ad: When responding to an ad, use the specific details about the ad to reference your letter. Be sure to include:

- the title of the job/position to be filled
- the name of the publication it appeared in

- the date
- reference number, if any

Don't make them guess what position you are interested in; state it specifically for them early on in the opening paragraph if you did not use the reference line to identify the job. Finish your paragraph by creatively giving a concrete benefit or skill you would bring to the job.

UL: If you are using an unsolicited approach, be sure to have done enough research to know the correct name of the position – the one they use in their company. What is called "Marketing Director" in one company may be "Marketing and Public Relations Project Manager" in another. Don't make them guess what position you want. It's not their job to figure out where you belong in their company, only **if** you belong. If you make them struggle to understand what you want, it's a surefire way to lose their attention immediately.

Importance in the Letter

It goes with saying – but we will anyway – that the importance of your opening paragraph is major! You can't skip it or avoid it, but you can do a half-hearted job and lessen your chances of success if done incorrectly.

Spend the needed time to write an interesting and stimulating opening. Don't take shortcuts here. Do your research.

Specifics

The opening is a paragraph of two to five sentences. Make it easy on your reader. Present your information in an easy-to-understand style that doesn't make the reader wonder what you are trying to say. Stay true to your own style, but be careful to not to bore or confuse your reader. Don't use a lot of jargon that isn't natural for you – it doesn't add to your letter, and the employer won't be impressed when they think they are getting a canned opening. Keep your sentences short – 12 to 15 words per sentence is usually enough.

Do This . . .

- Customize each letter to the specific employer you are contacting. Do not use mass-produced cover letters that make no differentiation from one company to another.
- Begin with an action-oriented sentence that relates to an issue or concern of the organization/company.
- Specify clearly your goals and/or the purpose or reason for your contact.

- Demonstrate that you did your homework prior to writing and that you raise only relevant points.

- Discuss a "hot" issue concerning the organization/company.

- Establish a link between the organization/company and yourself.

- Underline your interest in the organization/company.

- Describe a task to be achieved for which you possess the talents and the necessary competencies.

- Browse two or three magazines relating to the field/industry of the organization/company that you wish to approach. Look for two or three sentences, quotations, or items of specific information, which you believe will draw the attention of your reader. Select one to use. The purpose is to make the recipient WANT to read your entire letter.

- Use a search engine on the Internet to see what comes up. Enter several key words that are in direct relationship with the field/industry or the organization/company that you wish to contact. Try entering the name of the person you've addressed the letter to and see what information you can find. You will often be surprised by the amount of information listed about a person.

When appropriate:

- Mention the name of a common contact person that justifies your reason for writing. This is usually a strong selling point in your favor; place it right up front, but make sure you have the permission of the person you will name to do this.

- Mention a specific fact that relates directly to the person/department that you are approaching.

- Ask two or three friends/people whom you know and admire for their advice about your opening paragraph. When they are in agreement about the effectiveness of your opening, use it.

Don't Do This . . .

- Talk only about yourself.
- Make the focus of the letter about your needs and not theirs.
- Mention you are out of a job.
- Mention you are looking for a job – you are looking for a meeting.
- Leave out the title of the job for which you are applying.
- Write long paragraphs and endless sentences.

- Describe very obvious facts that will bore your reader.
- Criticize anything about the company, field, competition or customers, or your past employer(s).
- Use unnatural sounding jargon or job-speak.
- Assume a familiarity with your reader that you don't possess.
- Remain too general and confuse your reader.
- Use clichés.
- Use canned letters that are not personalized in any way to the specific person/company you are approaching.
- Have even one spelling mistake.

Examples of Mistakes to Avoid in Your Opening

Being Negative:

> "I have been let go and need a job badly."
> " I am at present unemployed ..."

Using Titles:

> "I am sure that my position as Head of Communications is going to interest you..."
> "I am a university graduate of Brightown University . . . . ."

Addressing Your Needs and Not Their Needs:

> "I have been looking for just the right job for many months, and think I have found it here with your company. I need to work and think this will give me the opportunity I have been seeking."

Making Value Judgments About the Company in a Negative Way:

> "I believe that your company has problems I can solve . . ."
> "I read that your company has a high turnover rate . . ."

Making Assumptions or Using Inappropriate Language:

> "I have the honor of replying to your ad and once you have read my letter I am sure you will want to hire me . . . ."
> "Will you grant me the benevolence of reading my letter... ?"
> "Paul, I am sure that you need my services."

Being Vague and Too Short:

> "I read your ad and would like to offer my services to your organization. Enclosed is my resume outlining my work history. Please call me at your earliest convenience to arrange an interview. I am most interested in joining your team. Thank you for your time." (entire letter)

Showing an Unchecked Ego:

> "I have two exceptional qualities: on the one hand ..."
> "You will never find another person with my special skills of ..."

Offering Unsubstantiated Statements About Yourself:

> "I was responsible for single-handedly turning my department around ..."
> "Over the last three years I have grown in my leadership skills and can now manage any number of employees ...."

Examples of Language Recommended for Your Opening

Ad:

> "I have recently read about your company in my local paper [list specifics of article]. I was particularly struck by the fact [name one fact]. I then saw your ad [ad specifics listed] and wanted to reply immediately. You specify that you are looking for a person who possesses 4 characteristics. Below is my summary on how I meet each characteristic."

> "This letter is in response to your ad, published in the ABC Times, dated November 11, 2004, for the position of Assistant Pharmacist, reference number 12345."

> "I have read your ad published in the ABC Times, dated November 11, 2004, for the position of Administrative Assistant, reference number 12345. I believe that I have the 4 qualifications you mentioned."

If you have mentioned in your reference line the name of the newspaper and ad details, you may start your letter by a paragraph grabbing your reader's attention, such as:

"During the last few days I have thought about the comments made by 4 of your customers about your delivery policy and offer my interpretation of them . . ."

"For the last 3 months, your organization/company has led an advertising campaign in more than 4 technical reviews. This advertisement mentions 5 advantages of your products versus your competition. I have found 2 more!"

"Were you impressed by the ad campaign for the local Breast Cancer Awareness Day, One Question, One Answer?"

UL:

Mention an article published in the press:

"In the May issue of THE INDUSTRIAL WORLD, Mr. Allan Smith talked about the threat of alternative commodities appearing on the market. This is the reason why I have decided to write to you."

"I read in the ABC Times that 72% of children like your new kind of pasta."

Use information found on a company's website:

"On your site, on the page dedicated to new applications of your special composites you mentioned 3 fields. I have found 2 additional new ones."

Relate your statement to a competitor – use tact and delicacy when trying this approach – never approach it negatively:

"The ABCD Company has decided to invest in the channel of microcomputers, and this is the reason I decided to send you this letter."

"During recent contacts with 5 companies in your field/industry, I noticed that school redistricting was a common concern to all of your competitors."

Using the referral of someone:

"Mr. Bob Smith, of Kline, Jones and Revere, mentioned to me only yesterday over lunch, that I would be an ideal match for the Marketing Manager position you currently have open and suggested I contact you immediately. He is familiar with my background and we have served together on the Board of Big Brothers for the past 2 years."

State a qualification or achievement:

"I developed a machine that can produce more than 70 forms, all different from one another."

"In the following paragraph I have outlined 2 alternatives which directly relate to 2 of your company's potential issues about [name them]*."*

Ask a question:

"Do you know a butcher's shop generating 22% of gross margin? In a supermarket in Anytown, this gross margin has varied from 20% to 26% in the last 2 years."

Chapter 15

Step 7: The Body of the Letter

Location in the Letter

The body of the letter is found after the opening paragraph and before the final follow-up paragraph.

John Smith
6 Hope Street
Anytown, CA 55555
555-123-4567

January 1, 20XX

Ms. Sue Jones
Production Manager
ABC Company
1234 First Street
Anytown, CA 55555

Dear Ms. Jones:

Your company has developed a unique safety device for wheelchairs that has only been copied by two competitors up to this time. I have thought of two additional ways to improve these wheelchairs that will make copying these safety devices very difficult.

I completed my studies as a mechanical technician at the ABC College last fall and have always been involved with concerns dealing with people who have physical limitations. I am currently active in a non-profit organization, which concentrates on access availability for wheelchairs in high-rise buildings in Anytown.

I have already had the opportunity to work on two projects while in college:

- Marketing: developed 17 technical brochures for a packaging company with $15 million in sales per year;
- Productivity: improved an assembly line for high tech products, resulting in a 17% growth in efficiency in one year.

I would welcome a call from you to set up a meeting. I can be reached at 555-123-4567.

Sincerely,

John Smith

Align to the left margin, but it may be moved to the right one tab when using the "Mirror" style (which will result in two columns). If using bullets, you will usually start with a left-aligned sentence or two, and then use bullets.

Reason and Purpose

Without this section, the writer has no way of outlining why an employer should be interested in them. The purpose of this section is to allow you to "make your case" well enough so an employer will want to meet with you to learn more. It is the main section of the letter and should be used to show, by giving quantifiable achievements and results, how you are qualified for the job. This is also the section to list pertinent educational degrees, certificates of completion, and other proof of your suitability for the job.

Ad: When responding to an ad, this section should be used to match, point for point, the criteria defining the job or the ideal candidate, and your qualifications that meet those criteria. For example, an ad lists these four criteria needed for the job:

- A Bachelor of Science Degree in Business
- A knowledge of the automobile industry
- Five years experience in after-sales service
- Willingness to travel

You must use the body of your letter to speak to each one of these criteria and how you match it. You can do that either in a traditional style with one or more paragraphs (sometimes using bullets to categorize each item), or you can use what we call the "mirror" technique, with two columns – one listing their criteria and the other stating how you meet the criteria.

UL: When writing an unsolicited letter, it becomes more difficult to know how to structure these one to three paragraphs. You have not been provided with an outline of skills needed or tasks to perform, so you must do some research. If you guess at this without benefit of any kind of reality check, you could be so far off the mark that you jeopardize the opportunity to impress your reader and then get invited in for a meeting. You must be clear enough about the job tasks, job content knowledge, skills needed, and other criteria for the job you seek that you can write about them intelligently. Three or four major characteristics should allow you to provide enough substance to write a meaningful letter.

You can gather the needed information by:

- Analyzing between 25 and 75 ads that correspond to the kind of position you seek, knowing that commonalities will show up.

- Meeting 3 to 5 people doing the kind of job you want and asking them to define the job characteristics and qualifications.
- Researching (the Internet is the easiest place to begin) the job title and noting what duties, tasks, and qualifications are typical for the kind of position you seek.

Once you have done some thorough research, you will have a good idea what to address in the body of your letter as the most important three or four characteristics. You may include a few more points if space permits, but do not try to cover everything – save some for a meeting.

Look back into your work history and find examples that show how you can match each characteristic. Only list actual achievements that had measurable and quantifiable results. This will demonstrate your ability to do the job.

Degree of Difficulty

As with the opening paragraph, which must grab the reader's interest and make them want to read the body of your letter, this section needs to be handled well. What you say here will determine your fate with the employer. You will either:

1. Be offered a meeting in the best-case.
2. Be sent a nice note or receive a polite call which says, in essence, "Good luck, but not with us."
3. Have the letter thrown out without acknowledgment of it in the worst-case scenario.

The only effective way to avoid #2 and #3 above, are to speak to the employer's needs and not your own. Through your research you should have identified what kind of issues the employer is facing and how you can help address those issues. Use this space to show how your qualifications, skills, abilities, and knowledge will help solve the issues. Offer concrete proof of how you are part of a solution, and not part of a problem. Feel confident that you possess the needed characteristics and be bold in your presentation of them, always keeping in mind the letter is for the benefit of the READER.

Present your relevant information in a clear, easy-to-understand style. Don't make your reader dig for your meaning or your value to them. Use clear sentences that show exactly what you are offering. Don't tell them something they already know; provide fresh thoughts, insights, and information. **Simplicity in the body of your letter will reduce its difficulty!**

Importance in the Letter

This item in the letter is essential and cannot be bypassed. The only real variable is how much you will choose to cover here and, hence, how long the body of your letter will be. Sometimes you will find that a single paragraph will be enough for your reader to decide if you should be called in for a meeting. You must select carefully what to cover here – if you can succinctly address their most pressing issue with your achievements, it will be enough. Sometimes you will need more space to develop your points. In no case should you write more than three to five paragraphs.

Specifics

The body will usually contain one or two well-written paragraphs. These paragraphs should be made up of three to seven short sentences – do not ramble on with 40-word sentences – 12 to 15 words per sentence is enough! Sometimes additional paragraphs will be needed. Do not assume a level of knowledge on the part of your reader that may not be there, so write as if you are speaking to someone who is not familiar with your topic.

Ad: When answering an ad using either a traditional style or the "You-Me-We" style, you will write your paragraphs in block form (bullets are okay here). Each paragraph will cover a different point that elaborates on your qualifications for the job.

- Candidate must have skills as a writer or editor

- Teaching credential with high school or college populations

- College degree, master's or higher

6 Hope Street
Anytown, CA 55555
555-123-4567

July 3, 20XX

Mr. Joe Black
Editorial Manager
ABC Publishing
1234 First Street
Anytown, CA 55555

RE: Your ad in the Sunday Times, dated July 1, 20XX, for a Proofreader, Job Number 5678Z

Dear Mr. Black:

The choice of a manuscript, the editing process, reproduction and distribution are the key tasks for the job of proofreader that you seek to fill. These tasks interest and excite me and that is why I am writing to you.

I think I am uniquely suited to this job based on these following qualifications.

Reviewer - My love of books and the written word prompted me to write reviews of the current fiction bestsellers for The Daily Press in Anytown. More recently, I have expanded these reviews to run in Everytown's Variety newspaper. I am fascinated by literature and interested in the process of how any book is published and in the care brought to its development.

Teaching Credential - I taught American and English Literature at the ABC High School in River City. This experience allowed me to share my passion with students who eventually managed to read an average of one book every two weeks, up from under one book per month.

Ph. D. in English Literature and Art History - I wrote an interdisciplinary report on English poet and engraver, William Blake, of the 16th century. I followed this up by editing the works of two of my colleagues, one paper on English literature, and one paper on art history. My attention to detail and my exacting concern for the proper use of words helped me to excel at these tasks.

As you requested I have enclosed my resume.

I would be happy to be able to develop these and other points with you during a meeting. I will call you next week to arrange a convenient date and time.

Sincerely,

Sue Jones

When using the "Mirror" style, you will list the characteristic from the ad on the left and place the "proof" of how you match that characteristic on the right.

Must have good social skills	*I know how to deal with people under stress . . .*
Must answer phones with a pleasant manner	*I handled 20 to 50 calls per hour . . .*
Must be bilingual	*I speak English and Spanish fluently . . .*

UL: When using an unsolicited approach, you may find a single paragraph will be enough. You must choose carefully and select something that will be convincing enough to stand alone. If you are not certain of the most pressing issue faced by your reader, it is better to develop your points over a few paragraphs. Begin the body of your letter with the most relevant or "hottest" topic and move down in importance in your next paragraph or two. It is certainly acceptable to use examples of your ability to do the job from both your work experience and your "extra-professional" experience (volunteering, leisure activities, special training programs attended, etc.).

Do This . . .

- Place yourself in the reader's shoes. What would you want to know?
- Customize the body of your letter to an individual employer. A one-size-fits-all doesn't work here (you've probably noticed it doesn't work so well for clothes either!).
- Use action verbs.
- List brief achievements, which correspond to their issues, where you:
  - effectively exercised responsibilities
  - were able to create and to innovate
  - produced concrete results
  - made decisions
- List achievements using quantifiable results.
- Write your numbers in figures; do not spell out numbers.
- Write only what pertains to their needs and interests; eliminate unimportant details.
- Write in short sentences that are easy to read and understand.
- Give only proof of what you can do; do not use platitudes and sweeping statements about yourself, boasting about what a "great" person you are – even if true!

- Place key words in **bold** text; do not overuse this effect. Three to seven bold words or phrases on any single page are enough.

- Present an idea or project that will grab their interest enough to call you for a meeting. Do not, however, give away all your secrets – save some for later (even in a meeting be careful with this – you do not want to give away the baby with the bath water – protect yourself).

- Use bullets when you list several points all pertaining to the same idea.

- Indent, if needed, to highlight a point.

- Put together at least 10 to 15 finished statements about your achievements and keep these handy to use when composing your letter. You can write them on index cards or the computer, using whatever system works best for you, and refer to them when writing your letter.

See Appendix A for more information on how to write achievement paragraphs.

Don't Do This . . .

- List achievements that have little or no bearing on the job and will therefore not interest the reader.

- Ask if they have a job you might fill. You then behave as a "Job-Beggar" and not a "Resource Person."

- Be vague, confused, or sloppy in your presentation.

- Pretend a "false humility" (*"Gee, shucks, it was nothing . . ."*)

- Adopt an arrogant attitude (*"I'm king/queen of the world . . ."*)

- Use a style which turns your letter into a slick "hard-selling sales" promotion. Your reader won't appreciate it and may feel offended. Nobody wants to feel they are being "sold" – it belittles them.

- Use clichés or platitudes or quotes, which are mostly showy, usually meaningless, and don't originate from you. If you are not the author of what you say, leave it for another time.

- Say, **EVER**, *"As you can see from my resume . . ."* They can read the resume; do not waste your valuable space regurgitating points from it.

- Be overly general, which is meaningless, or overly specific by getting mired in minutiae. If what you say is not easily understood, the reader won't bother to figure it out.

- Repeat yourself.

- List skills or qualifications without offering substantiation of them.

- Apologize for yourself in any way.

- Offer negative comments about anyone, especially past employers or their competition.

- Play on the reader's empathy or sympathy by telling a hard-luck story.

- Give personal details that have no bearing on the job and tell the reader more than they ever wanted to know.

- Talk about salary or benefits. That is best left for a meeting where negotiation can take place after a job offer.

- Tell them what they cannot do, such as contact your current employer.

- Make demands on them.

- Tell them who else you are contacting for a meeting, or who else has already rejected you.

- Talk only about them, and not about yourself. It is good to bring up a point or two about the employer/company/person, but you must include relevant information about yourself if you hope to interest them enough call you for a meeting.

- Tell the employer what is wrong with their company and how you are the person to "fix" it. They will not appreciate hearing:
  - They have problems
  - You want to point them out
  - You are the one to fix those problems, above all other people who already work there
  - You have a negative mindset rather than a positive one

Consider carefully if you want to contact an employer. If you do not feel inspired by the job, this will show through in your letter – these things are subtle. Don't waste precious energy and time when you don't feel enthusiasm and excitement about a job. It is a disservice to yourself and the employer.

Examples of Mistakes to Avoid in the Body of the Letter

Telling Them Their Problems:

"I noticed from an article I read in Forbes Magazine (Oct. 2004), that your company has lost an 8% market share in the last year. I understand the forces that created this downturn and feel I can help you with your problem. I think you should . . . ."

Being Vague and Unfocused:

"Although I have no previous working experience for the job you advertised, or for working in a company the size of yours, I think my other qualities will more than make up for this lack of relevant experience. If enthusiasm and organizational skills count for anything, I am your man. Enclosed please find a current resume."

Apologizing for Yourself:

"I am sorry that I do not have all the qualifications you requested in your ad, but I think you will find I would still be a good candidate for the job."

"While my work history is stellar, I have had some personal issues to deal with over the past few years which have made it impossible for me to consider a new job. I regret that part of my life, but it is over and I am ready to move on now."

Being Boastful or Arrogant:

"The ABC Company had a problem in terms of delay in its after-sale service. I approached it and managed to master it quickly, thanks to my will and my enthusiasm."

"I have enclosed a copy of my resume that outlines my skills and experience. I know I am the ideal candidate for this job. I will be an asset to your company. Do yourself a favor and call me for an interview."

Being Too Humble:

"We managed to overcome the computer problem that had plagued the company for months. I would like to take credit for this, but it was mostly due to the efforts of my team. While I was their leader, they showed amazing creativity and innovation in their approach."

Making Demands on the Prospective Employer:

"I noticed, after looking at other similar jobs in similar companies, that your pay scale is toward the low end of the range. I must ask you to consider revising it toward the upper end of the range."

"Tell me how I can be the one to get this job."

"I demand that you pay me in cash only. I do not have a bank account at this time."

"Do not overlook this opportunity I am presenting to you. Grant me an interview! Soon!"

Talking All About Yourself:

"I am very interested in applying for your internship program. I think it will be an amazing opportunity. I am currently a student at ABC University, majoring in Social Welfare. I have done a lot of speaking on this topic and I have written many short articles on how we can overcome poverty in our cities. I have very strong communication skills. I am good at dealing with people, regardless of their background and heritage. I am a hard worker. I am excited to go to work every day." **(Nine "I"s)**

Giving Details That are Irrelevant and Are Too Personal in Nature:

"I am a mother of three wonderful children who are now in school during the day. I would like to return to the workforce . . . ."

"I retired last year and found that I do not like sitting around the house all day. I know that I am over 65, but feel I still have a lot to offer to an employer."

Using Cutesy Quotes or Clichés:

"'Choose a job you love, and you will never have to work a day in your life.' Don't you agree with this quote from Confucius? I do and that is why I have chosen to write to you. You have the job that I would love to do."

"Can you see yourself on top of the world? That's where I will be if you are kind enough to grant me an interview!"

"When life gives you lemons, make lemonade. That's my philosophy of life. I think you will see from my enclosed resume that I've done that at every turn."

"'When God closes a door somewhere, he opens a window someplace else.' You are my 'window.'"

Playing on Sympathy or Mentioning Personal Issues:

"When I saw your advertisement for an office manager, I was delighted. I have spent the last two years of my life taking care of my sick mother, who recently

passed away. She was a wonderful person who deserved better than she got. I am now ready to work again, as my burden is over."

"It was not my fault that I have had to spend the last several years in rehab. I was hit broadside by another car in 2002 and have spent my time recovering from that accident. My doctor says I am now ready to resume working, so I hope you will consider me."

Listing Unrelated Qualifications:

"I know this job calls for a person who can analyze data from a wide range of sources and find common denominators. I would like to say that I think my ability to 'see the forest for the trees' is a much more valuable skill in the long run."

"You have stated you need a person who is willing to travel. While I can't do that, I can say with some assurance that I will be able to get the job done in a timely fashion. I have always excelled at being a 'quick study' and usually am up and running within a week or two."

Telling Them What They Can't Do:

"I have worked for the ABC Company for the last two years. I would ask that you do not contact them, however, for personal reasons."

Using Bad Grammar or Making Spelling Mistakes:

"I worked for over fiteen years for the XYZ in Anytown, CA. I think if you were to inquire with them about my long years of service, they would tell you that I was an explarary employee and never missed a day of work. I was always on time and rarely late. I can promise you the same kind of dedication and loyaty."

"I think you will notice from my resume, my dedicaton and service to my last four employers was explemenatary."

Mentioning Rejections From Others:

"I have offered my services to ABC Company as well as yourself, and while they did not have an opening for someone with my background at this time, I am hopeful that you will."

Examples of Achievement Language
Recommended for the Body of the Letter

"Using 2 simple approaches, I managed to reduce the delay of the after-service from 17 days to 4 days at the ABC Company. I did this heading a team of 5 people."

"I offer 3 examples of fund-raising operations, which I led for charitable organizations, similar in size to your company."

"I managed the office for 4 doctors and supervised a staff of over 20 people. Policies I put into place for childcare and flexible hours reduced our turnover rate by 6% in the first 2 years of my tenure."

"Responsible for all marketing functions in the catalog sales department, I revised our 4 annual catalogs and incorporated over 40 new products. Sales in the first year after revision were up by 14%."

"Contributed to a weekly column in our local paper about the real estate market and sales trends and spoke to groups on a monthly basis about these topics. Readership of the paper increased by 11% over a 6-month period."

"In my function as a Student Services Coordinator, I oversaw recruitment and retention services for new and continuing students. My program for continuing students called 'What Can Your School Do for You?' was attended by over half of the 2,000 students enrolled, in the first year of its operation."

"Designed over 10 new web sites as a freelance artist in the last 6 months, with a 1-month turnaround time for the client. 2 of these sites were mentioned in the 'ABC Journal of Web Design' in the December 15th, 2004 edition."

"As a labor relations manager, I prepared information used by management during negotiations that resulted in a fair outcome for employees and a $1.12/hour raise for entry-level positions."

"With responsibilities for monthly inventories, payroll, supply ordering, and personnel recruitment, I managed a 22-person insurance office. I was able to eliminate redundancy in several of our systems, which resulted in a 4.5% savings on consumable products and a 5.5% savings on fees paid to outside payroll services."

"I have already had the opportunity to work on 2 projects while in college:

- *Marketing: developed 12 technical brochures for a packaging company with $15 million in sales per year.*
- *Productivity: improved an assembly line for high-tech products, resulting in a 17% growth in efficiency in one year."*

"In the last 5 years, I have been coordinator of a 32-team softball league and have been the chairperson for 2 large charity fundraisers to benefit organizations in my community, raising over $125,000 on average each year."

"As a travel consultant for Higher Learning Tours, I worked for many years as a lecturer and guide, participating in over 35 different tours."

36 More Examples of Achievement Paragraphs By Category

Administration

I streamlined the filing system for over 2,000 personnel records, allowing any record to be accessed within seconds. I was awarded a certificate of merit from my employer for this work.

As administrative director of ABC Company, I managed to improve the gross margin of our company by 2%. This was done with the cooperation of the staff manager by applying a new method to the negotiation agreements.

The ABC Company entrusted me to reorganize its administrative procedures. Assisted by a secretary, within 2 months we had instituted 7 successful new methods which saved 20% on time needed to execute daily tasks.

In four days I set up a system to archive over 1,200 index cards. This allowed necessary information to be found with 5 fewer steps than before.

I volunteered to put all documents from the company into a word processing program on the computer. At the end of 2 months when the job was completed, the time needed to find any document was reduced by 50%. I completed this project without compromising my usual tasks.

Audit

By performing a study using an integrated approach, I demonstrated that a $10,000,000 division of a leading chemical group in Europe had no profit potential in its market. As a result, the division was closed.

Computers

Leading a team of 6, we succeeded in eliminating computer database crashes that were very costly to the company, saving $40,000 per month. This problem was long standing, but practical solutions had never been found. I brought together a diverse team of specialists, developed an innovative action plan, and managed the project through to completion.

Consulting

I managed various engineering consulting studies of over $15,000,000 in value. I faced and successfully overcame logistic, political, and organizational difficulties operating in the Far East.

I was able to achieve a significant increase in my personal fee rate (+ 145%) during my 2 years as a healthcare consultant, despite recession, aggressive price competition, and sales force pressure.

Control

I reduced overspending from a historically high level of $500,000 to $100,000. As part of a team of 3, we improved communication with factory management.

Development

I set up a new unit with 4 staff people. Important success factors included an increase of 17% in revenue and an improvement in internal and external client satisfaction, which was raised from 5.2 to 7.4, on a scale of 10.

Finance

I identified the tangible means to increase the financial results in an engineering firm by 50%. This led to a refinancing of this company by a group of investors who were convinced by my recommendations.

I was responsible for managing $50,000,000 of taxable bond portfolios. I achieved a performance of 100 basis points above the index in light of political uncertainty.

With a group of 4 members, I contributed to the set-up of a portfolio of new customers, representing yearly revenues of $1,200,000. I initiated and completed 7 transactions in excess of $250,000 each, in a declining market.

Management

I managed to reduce the average project development time from 6 months to 3 months. I created a training program and improved communication among the 12 members of my team.

Marketing

As product manager responsible for 2 different market segments, I succeeded in improving our market share by 18%. This was done in an increasingly competitive environment within an 8-month period.

In my position in the U.S. headquarters while working as an R&D analyst, my team of 3 managed to negotiate an exclusive distribution agreement with another U.S. company. The negotiation took one year to be completed and opened a new market segment in Europe for the company. Sales now represent more than $16,000,000 per year.

I co-created an entertainment placement agency in a country that, in 2003, claimed a 12% unemployment rate. I trained and placed 31 entertainers and negotiated contracts with 7 resorts.

Operations

I managed a team of 12 people to implement a management system in a manufacturing company that had 8 regional plants. This saved $900,000 every 4 months, due to purchasing and inventory consolidation.

Production

In a manufacturing workshop, I managed to increase productivity by 15%. I was helped by 2 technical experts and used 2 modem-optimizing tests.

I led team of 4 engineers in preparing for production of packaging machines in Anytown. As a result, production has started on schedule.

With a team of 7 people, we reduced the plant's need for external contracts by 22%. This required a change in traditional working practices.

Production Control

I introduced engineering procedures to 17 very experienced foremen and workers, mixing human relations, politics, and engineering. I succeeded without causing any conflict.

Project Management

I managed a project to renew all returnable packaging. The activities of 3 suppliers and 5 departments had to be closely coordinated due to limited time availability. Within 3 months we succeeded in starting the distribution of 5 million new packages into the market.

Quality Control

As head of the Project department, I was responsible for developing and implementing a new project management methodology, compliant with the International Standards Organization (ISO) 9000 quality standard. This methodology was developed within the time and budget limits allocated. After 1 year of use, it increased observed customer satisfaction by 30%.

R&D

I doubled the rate of first quality production for a technical product subject to many different and specific requirements. I initiated 4 different types of procedures, which were utilized by a department of 80 people.

I invented, developed, and launched 2 new services. After 2 years they now represent 34% of the turnover of this organization.

I was in charge of an R&D study for the latest fighter aircraft. The budget was $500,000, and with the help of 2 other engineers we created software to simulate a low altitude flight. The software was completed successfully and was used to determine the size of the highly expensive on-board computer.

I decreased the per-unit container cost by 20% by development of an automated system and a new set of procedures. I was assisted by a team of 14 IS people.

I developed a method for a lifetime forecast for a specific product. I coordinated 3 R&D teams. The method is now used for all products that are based on the same technology.

Sales

In 2 years, I tripled export sales to Latin American subsidiaries of an Anytown laboratory. I used a new international communication system.

I invented, developed, and launched 2 new services. After 2 years, they now represent 34% of the sales of this organization.

Strategic Planning

Working in a team of 8 people, we persuaded the Chairman and Board not to acquire a company costing $550,000,000. This target company's share price has halved since our recommendation.

The price of our main article has increased 3-fold. This resulted in an increase of gross profits from $12,000.000 to $21,000,000 in 3 years.

Taxes

I succeeded in reducing our tax bill on vehicles by 20%. I did this by creating a new information system and replacing the old archaic way. This had not been tried before due to the complexity of the algorithms involved in the calculation.

Training

I created a series of marketing seminars for the 350+ sales people working in our organization. After some expected resistance from these departments, this series has been adopted as an annual event in different locations around the country.

Location in the Letter

This is the last paragraph of text in your letter and follows directly after the body of the letter. It is above the complimentary closing.

John Smith
6 Hope Street
Anytown, CA 55555
555-123-4567

January 1, 20XX

Ms. Sue Jones
Production Manager
ABC Company
1234 First Street
Anytown, CA 55555

Dear Ms. Jones:

Your company has developed a unique safety device for wheelchairs that has only been copied by two competitors up to this time. I have thought of two additional ways to improve these wheelchairs that will make copying these safety devices very difficult.

I completed my studies as a mechanical technician at the ABC College last fall and have always been involved with concerns dealing with people who have physical limitations. I am currently active in a non-profit organization, which concentrates on access availability for wheelchairs in high-rise buildings in Anytown.

I have already had the opportunity to work on two projects while in college:

- Marketing: developed 17 technical brochures for a packaging company with $15 million in sales per year;
- Productivity: improved an assembly line for high tech products, resulting in a 17% growth in efficiency in one year.

I will call you on the 15th of January to inquire about a meeting. I can be reached at 555-123-4567.

Sincerely,

John Smith

Reason and Purpose

This paragraph is extremely important because you will use it to finish up the letter and suggest the process for follow-up. You want to capitalize on the interest that your preceding paragraphs may have generated. You have outlined why they would be justified in spending some more time with you to see if there is a good match between you and the job/company. You now need to make the most of that by setting some kind of "follow-up" or "next step" arrangements.

You can take one of four approaches to do this:

1. You can place yourself in the reactive or passive or pessimistic position by suggesting:

    "If you are interested, please contact me at . . ."

    We don't recommend this style, as an **"If" opens the door to a "No"**! This approach will leave all the power and initiative in the hands of the employer.

2. You can place yourself in the reactive or reserved position by suggesting:

    "I am at your disposal to develop these points during a meeting on . . ."

    This approach also leaves the power and initiative for follow-up in the hands of the employer.

3. You can place yourself in the active or proactive position by suggesting:

    "I will call you on Tuesday, January 2nd, to set up a time for a meeting."

    This will place you in the driver's seat and give you the initiative to handle the responsibility for follow-up.

4. You can use the "In Your Area" approach when job hunting in an area different from where you live by suggesting:

    "I will be in Anytown for a meeting over the week of February 1st to 5th and would welcome the chance to talk further with you. I will call you on January 15th to see if we can find a mutually convenient time for a meeting."

This approach helps both you and the employer understand the opportunity created by your visit to their area. It is very limited in its time frame and calls for an immediate decision to take advantage of circumstances.

Degree of Difficulty

The difficulty with this paragraph is not so much in the form it should take, but in the underlying attitude that many job hunters have about how they are perceived by the employer if they ask for a meeting.

There are two basic underlying thoughts that fuel this attitude:

- Job hunters may assume that the employer will be so impressed with their letter that they will call to set up a meeting, and the job hunter can sit back and wait for their call.

- Conversely, and at the other end of that spectrum, is the belief some job hunters hold that the employer will be so unimpressed with their letter that they shouldn't risk the presumption of asking for a meeting.

Both ways of thinking do a great disservice to the job hunter and the employer. There is so much assumption involved in both. With assumption comes the possibility for mistakes, misevaluations, and missed chances.

In the first case, it's a "risky" proposition, and perhaps a bit egotistical, to bank on the employer having the time, energy, and interest to seek you out above all others.

In the second case, it's an "insecure" stance by the job hunter that they don't have the necessary value and qualifications for the employer to even bother with them.

It is better to look at it logically. The employer needs something and you need something. If you must assume anything, always assume that it will be a win/win situation. Feeling energized by that belief, you will feel better, get more positive results, and increase your chance for success.

Importance in the Letter

It's hard to do much of anything without a plan! Conscious thought and energy have to go into making something – anything – happen. It's as true for the trivial or menial tasks in our lives as it is the important and meaningful tasks in our lives. So, we need to take responsibility for the process of trying to get what we want.

This means a cover letter must make some provision for the "next step" or "follow-up." It isn't sufficient to write a nice letter about how you might be just the person the company needs and then leave it there, although many job hunters do exactly that. You must methodically and precisely outline how the opportunity for further conversation could happen. You may not control the final outcome, but you have to take responsibility by suggesting the "next step" – a call to action.

Be proactive and say when you will contact the employer to see if they have more interest in you. The importance of this cannot be understated. **If you leave this out, you have no means to get back in touch with the employer gracefully and professionally**.

If you use the more reserved approach and suggest you are eager for them to contact you, the call to action is in their hands.

You may sometimes wish to include both of these options. You can tell the employer you are eagerly anticipating their call and remain available for that AND that you will call them at an appointed time.

Specifics

This paragraph may begin with one or two sentences as a "summarization" or "wrap-up" to the body of your letter. Do not repeat what you have already said, however. You may then use two to three sentences to outline the follow-up process.

Do This . . .

- In your first sentence or two of the paragraph, summarize your value to the organization. Confirm your interest in the job.

- Specify that you are taking the initiative for the follow-up.

- Suggest a short meeting. Let them know you are not asking for hours of their time. Say how many minutes, i.e., "*a 20-minute meeting . . .*"

- Be sure to suggest a person-to-person meeting as the ultimate goal.

- Suggest alternatives for follow-up. Make it easy for the employer to see you.

- Write a clear and concise action plan.

- Be explicit about how follow-up will occur – a call, letter, email, etc.
- Be flexible about times you can meet.
- Use words like *"to speak more about"* or *"to discuss in more detail."*

Don't Do This . . .

- Adopt an inflexible attitude about how things must go.
- Offer only one time or date for follow-up.
- Ask for a long meeting.
- Suggest a telephone interview – it's a quick and, for the employer, fairly painless way to screen you out.
- Be vague or unclear about what you want or will do.
- Betray an attitude of arrogance ("of course, they will want me").
- Forget to specify the purpose of a meeting.
- Raise limits or constraints about what days or hours you are available to meet.
- Use the word "if," which opens the door to the word "no."
- Use conditional language, such as *"in case this letter catches your interest."*
- Use a call for hope – *"Hoping that this letter proves interesting to you."*
- Sound overly anxious or apprehensive in tone.

Examples of Mistakes to Avoid in Your "Follow-Up" Paragraph

Writing Nothing About Follow-Up:

"Hoping my letter will impress upon you the extent to which I desire to work for your company."

Leaving Follow-Up in the Hands of the Recipient, With No Way for You to Get Back into the Process:

"I am sure my letter will grab your attention and convince you that I should be called in for an interview."

"I would love the pleasure of speaking with you in more detail about my many accomplishments. I will wait for your call to arrange a meeting."

"After reading my letter, it is my sincere hope that you will want to meet with me. I am available for an interview at any time."

Adopting an Attitude You Are Not Worth the Time for an Interview:

"I am sure your calendar is full, but I would be very appreciative if you could grant me a few minutes of your time, which would be a great honor to me."

Examples of Language to Use in Your "Follow-Up" Paragraph

You can outline your intention to call and list a very specific date and time. On the one hand, it is good to set up specifics so the employer will know what to expect and to keep yourself on track. This has a professional feel to it and leaves you with options.

On the other hand, it is sometimes wiser to leave the time and date of your follow-up call more open, so that the employer doesn't alert his assistant/secretary to screen you out. When you call, you can say, "I mentioned I would call soon to set up an appointment." This will keep an element of surprise on your side, while still showing your initiative.

"I will call you within the next ten days to see when you might be able to meet with me to further discuss the points I have outlined above."

"I would be most happy to develop one of the above points during a meeting with you at your convenience. I will call you to see when that would be possible."

"I will call you on June 1st, in the morning, to find out a time that might be mutually beneficial for a meeting to further explore your needs."

I would welcome a call from you to set up a meeting. Should I miss your call, I will take the initiative to call you during the first week of June."

"I am most interested in the opportunity to work with you. I will be in your area from June 1st to June 5th and would welcome a chance to come by and meet with you. I will call you next week to see when you have an opening."

"Thank you very much for considering me a serious candidate. I believe I have the skills you need to help move your Public Relations department to the next level. I would love to develop these ideas with you in a meeting. I will call you on June 5th to see when that could happen."

"Please feel free to contact me at any time so I may clarify or expand on my comments herein. I can be reached at 555-1234 during working hours. As

it happens, I will be in your area next month and would welcome the chance to come by your office for a short visit. After June 12th, I will give you a call to follow up."

For email:

"I have attached two documents which will further highlight my interest in your company. Please feel free to call me if you have trouble opening these attachments, and I will resend them in another format. I would welcome the chance to discuss the ideas contained in them with you. I will call you next week to see what can be arranged."

Chapter 17

Step 9: The Complimentary Closing

Location in the Letter

This item follows the last paragraph in your letter and comes directly before your signature.

If using Full Block style, it will be aligned to the left margin. If using Modified Block style, it will be aligned in the middle of the page.

Full Block

John Smith
6 Hope Street
Anytown, CA 55555
555-123-4567

January 1, 20XX

Ms. Sue Jones
Production Manager
ABC Company
1234 First Street
Anytown, CA 55555

Dear Ms. Jones:

Your company has developed a unique safety device for wheelchairs that has only been copied by two competitors up to this time.

I completed my studies as a mechanical technician at the ABC College last fall and have always been involved with concerns dealing with people who have physical limitations. I am currently active in a non-profit organization, which concentrates on access availability for wheelchairs in high-rise buildings in Anytown.

I have already had the opportunity to work on two projects while in college:

- Marketing: developed 17 technical brochures for a packaging company with $15 million in sales per year;
- Productivity: improved an assembly line for high tech products, resulting in a 17% growth in efficiency in one year.

I would welcome a call from you to set up a meeting. I can be reached at 555-123-4567.

Sincerely,

John Smith

Modified Block

John Smith
6 Hope Street
Anytown, CA 55555
555-123-4567

January 1, 20XX

Ms. Sue Jones
Production Manager
ABC Company
1234 First Street
Anytown, CA 55555

Dear Ms. Jones:

Your company has developed a unique safety device for wheelchairs that has only been copied by two competitors up to this time. I have thought of two additional ways to improve these wheelchairs that will make copying these safety devices very difficult.

I completed my studies as a mechanical technician at the ABC College last fall and have always been involved with concerns dealing with people who have physical limitations. I am currently active in a non-profit organization, which concentrates on access availability for wheelchairs in high-rise buildings in Anytown.

I have already had the opportunity to work on two projects while in college:

- Marketing: developed 17 technical brochures for a packaging company with $15 million in sales per year;
- Productivity: improved an assembly line for high tech products, resulting in a 17% growth in efficiency in one year.

I would welcome a call from you to set up a meeting. I can be reached at 555-123-4567.

Sincerely,

John Smith

Reason and Purpose

The good news is that when you reach this item, you have finished the hardest part of your letter! The closing, usually called complimentary because it is meant to close the letter in a pleasant fashion, is a matter of politeness and etiquette.

Degree of Difficulty

There should be nothing terribly difficult about this item. The only questions are those of tone and the degree of formality you wish to adopt for the letter. If you try for something original and catchy, you will spend many minutes looking for just the right words. We think your time is better spent elsewhere. Don't worry on this point; the reader will only glance at it and move on.

Importance in the Letter

The importance of this item is only noticed if you bypass it and don't write any kind of closing, or if you try to write some meaningful and original closing sentence that goes on too long. A short closing is preferable to a longer one.

Specifics

It is often sufficient to use just one or two words. There are several very traditional complimentary closings commonly used for cover letters that work just fine. A comma is used as punctuation.

Do This . . .

- Err on the side of a more formal tone, especially when you don't know the person to whom you are writing.

- If you are in doubt, "Sincerely" is a common and often-used closing. Its tone is slightly less formal, but it is still professional.

Don't Do This . . .

- Be too familiar and use an overly friendly tone.

- Ignore the basic rules of politeness and etiquette by leaving it out.

- Try to say too much here. It is better to add any miscellaneous thoughts to your last paragraph or a well-thought out postscript.

- Use slang, like *"Catch you later, baby!"*

- Adopt the formula of the last century, which consisted of up to three lines of text for the closing.

- Use the wrong punctuation.

Examples of Mistakes to Avoid in Your Closing

Leave the Closing Out Altogether

Being Too Long and Too Formal:

"In the terms of this letter I ask you to receive, Madam, the expression of my feelings of deep respect and admiration."

"Thank you for the care and the attention which you will indeed want to offer to this letter so I ask you to approve, Sir, the expression of my most sincere feelings."

Being Too informal:

"Thanks!"

"Best,"

"See you!"

Phrases that would be better put in the last paragraph of letter than used for a complimentary closing:

"With warmest regards and hope for a meeting in the future."

"I thank you in advance for reading my letter."

Examples of Language Recommended for Your Closing

Formal tone –"Respectfully yours,"

Standard closing –"Sincerely,"

Typical but less formal than "Respectfully yours" –"Sincerely yours,"

Polite –"Very truly yours,"

Polite – "Yours truly,"

Friendly – "Cordially yours,"

Thoughtful and friendly –"Best wishes," or "Best regards,"

Chapter 18

Step 10: The Signature

Location in the Letter

The signature follows the complimentary closing and consists of two parts.

You will need to leave a block of space – four lines are usually recommended– for your actual signature. You may leave only two or three lines if leaving a full four lines would cause your letter to spill over onto two pages.

After this space, you will type your name, as you want it to read and sign above this line in the block of space you have left open.

The signature block is above the Enclosures line or postscript line. If using neither of those, it will be the last item on your letter.

If using Full Block style, it will be aligned to the left margin. If using Modified Block style, it will be aligned under the complimentary closing in the middle of the page. The closing and signature block should always be aligned together. Do not place one to the left and the other to the middle.

Full Block

John Smith
6 Hope Street
Anytown, CA 55555
555-123-4567

January 1, 20XX

Ms. Sue Jones
Production Manager
ABC Company
1234 First Street
Anytown, CA 55555

Dear Ms. Jones:

Your company has developed a unique safety device for wheelchairs that has only been copied by two competitors up to this time. I have thought of two additional ways to improve these wheelchairs that will make copying these safety devices very difficult.

I completed my studies as a mechanical technician at the ABC College last fall and have always been involved with concerns dealing with people who have physical limitations. I am currently active in a non-profit organization, which concentrates on access availability for wheelchairs in high-rise buildings in Anytown.

I have already had the opportunity to work on two projects while in college:

- Marketing: developed 17 technical brochures for a packaging company with $15 million in sales per year;
- Productivity: improved an assembly line for high tech products, resulting in a 17% growth in efficiency in one year.

I would welcome a call from you to set up a meeting. I can be reached at 555-123-4567.

Sincerely,

John Smith

John Smith

Modified Block

John Smith
6 Hope Street
Anytown, CA 55555
555-123-4567

January 1, 20XX

Ms. Sue Jones
Production Manager
ABC Company
1234 First Street
Anytown, CA 55555

Dear Ms. Jones:

Your company has developed a unique safety device for wheelchairs that has only been copied by two competitors up to this time. I have thought of two additional ways to improve these wheelchairs that will make copying these safety devices very difficult.

I completed my studies as a mechanical technician at the ABC College last fall and have always been involved with concerns dealing with people who have physical limitations. I am currently active in a non-profit organization, which concentrates on access availability for wheelchairs in high-rise buildings in Anytown.

I have already had the opportunity to work on two projects while in college:

- Marketing: developed 17 technical brochures for a packaging company with $15 million in sales per year;
- Productivity: improved an assembly line for high tech products, resulting in a 17% growth in efficiency in one year.

I would welcome a call from you to set up a meeting. I can be reached at 555-123-4567.

Sincerely,

John Smith

John Smith

Reason and Purpose

It is common courtesy to sign your name, showing that you have written the letter and, in essence, taken credit for it.

Degree of Difficulty

In one respect, it could be said that the signature is the easiest part of the letter. It's your name, you sign it, and you're done. You do it a thousand times a year. But on closer examination, it can also prove to be an issue if your handwriting isn't good, comprehensible, or legible. You will need to practice writing clearly if this is the case.

Additionally, you will need to decide if adding a title is appropriate. Sometimes it is fine to add a title when it is relevant. At other times the addition of a title may be too formal and cause the reader to think you are pretentious, arrogant, or self-important.

Importance in the Letter

If your letter is being mailed the traditional way, you should make certain to sign it. Leaving it unsigned shows a lack of attention to detail and will cause the reader to wonder why you didn't bother to sign it. Be attentive and verify that you have signed your letter.

If you are sending your letter via email, it becomes more difficult to sign the letter unless you have signature-generating software. If you do not, you will have to send the letter without the handwritten signature. In this case, you do not need to leave four spaces between the closing and the typed name. One or two will be sufficient.

Specifics

This is generally one line. Your name should be signed exactly as you have typed it. If you have added a title, you should write the title directly after the signature, separating the two with a comma.

If you have had someone else type your letter for you, typically you would include these identification initials just below the typed signature. Common styles are:

- FBH/jr
- DP:jf
- jrf

The writer's initials are placed in capitals, followed by a slash or colon, and then the initials of the person who produced the letter are given in lowercase. Alternatively, occasionally just the initials of the person who typed the letter (who is not the author of it) will be given in lowercase. Any of the three styles is acceptable.

Do This . . .

- Use black or blue ink to sign your name. Make sure your pen is clean and will not leave a big smudge of ink when you first start to write.

- Be sure to type your name as you use it in business. The name should match exactly the name on your letterhead or your resume if you are sending one with the letter.

- Sign your name exactly as you have typed it on the letter.

- If you are adding a title, keep it short. Write it directly after your signature, separating them with a comma.

- Make sure your writing is legible. It does not have to be fancy script, but the reader should be able to read it well enough to know what it is. Imagine the reader did not have the benefit of the typed name below to decipher it.

Don't Do This . . .

- Forget to sign your letter.

- Sign or type only your first name. Use your entire name.

- Sign using a nickname.

- Use colored ink – like red, green, purple, or orange!

- Draw "smiley faces" by your signature. Do not add graphics of any kind to the signature block in an effort to make yourself more familiar and seemingly relaxed.

- Scan your signature or use a stamp signature if you are sending a traditional letter. Write it out on each letter.

Examples of Mistakes to Avoid With Your Signature

Illegible:

Only Initials:

Examples Recommended for Your Signature

The three characteristics that are judged in a signature, albeit subconsciously, are:

- its legibility
- its seriousness
- its balance

Location in the Letter

Reference to enclosures follows below the typed signature line or identification initials if used, and is directly above the postscript line, if used. Space two lines before typing the enclosure line. You may space only one line if, by spacing two, your letter will move to two pages in length.

Align with the left margin.

John Smith
6 Hope Street
Anytown, CA 55555
555-123-4567

January 1, 20XX

Ms. Sue Jones
Production Manager
ABC Company
1234 First Street
Anytown, CA 55555

Dear Ms. Jones:

Your company has developed a unique safety device for wheelchairs that has only been copied by two competitors up to this time.

I completed my studies as a mechanical technician at the ABC College last fall and have always been involved with concerns dealing with people who have physical limitations. I am currently active in a non-profit organization, which concentrates on access availability for wheelchairs in high-rise buildings in Anytown.

I have already **had the** opportunity to work on two projects while in college:

- Marketing: developed 17 technical brochures for a packaging company with $15 million in sales per year;
- Productivity: improved an assembly line for high tech products, resulting in a 17% growth in efficiency in one year.

I would welcome a call from you to set up a meeting. I can be reached at 555-123-4567.

Sincerely,

John Smith

John Smith

Enclosures (3)

Reason and Purpose

The notation of enclosures is necessary when you send other documents with your letter. This notation alerts your reader that additional material is included with the letter, or attached if your letter is sent via email. This is also the area of the letter to note if the letter is being copied to others by using the "cc:" notation.

Ad: When answering an ad, you may include documents with your letter. A resume may be enclosed or other documents you want the employer to see that pertain to your application. It is here that you will list either the number of documents enclosed – i.e., (3) – or list each document by name – i.e., *Resume, Article from the ABC Times, dated 11/11/01*, etc.

UL: When using an unsolicited approach, you may choose to skip this item and send just the letter itself. If you have done your job well with the letter, it should be sufficient to stand alone and spur their interest enough to call you for a meeting. It can be dangerous to include a resume at this point, as the information contained in it may be more harmful than helpful and cause you to be screened out prematurely. However, you may find it sensible to send other kinds of documents that support your application. These might include photographs (not of yourself, however, unless you are a model or actor!), a floor plan (if you are an architect, for example), an article about yourself, the company, or the industry, or others types of documents which add weight to your case but are not confidential.

Degree of Difficulty

This item is not particularly difficult, as the text of your letter should have outlined what documents are enclosed with the letter. You must include all documents you mentioned in the letter, so you do not appear disorganized or lacking in attention to detail. The form to do this is relatively uncomplicated, so it does not present any difficulties.

Importance in the Letter

This is an optional item and depends on what you stated in the body of your letter. If you did not mention sending other documents with your letter, you may bypass this item.

This item will also depend if you are responding to an ad or using an unsolicited approach.

Ad: Traditionally, most people attached a resume with their letter when responding to an ad. While this is standard practice, you may wish to consider withholding the resume until a meeting is scheduled. If your letter proves interesting enough, your new potential boss or line manager might call you if they like what they see. These are the best people to know what the job requires and how you might be able to fill the bill. If you attach a resume, there is a good chance that your letter will be directed immediately to a personnel manager or human resources person. These folks, while good intentioned, may not be as well acquainted with the qualifications for the job and screen your application out before it has a chance to get to the person who could best evaluate what you are offering. They will screen you out because your resume gives information that has not been asked for in the ad. You have given them more information to use "against" you, rather than "for" you.

If you do attach a resume, be sure to list it on the enclosure line.

UL: If you write an unsolicited letter, it is best not to include a resume. You are looking for a meeting to further explore possibilities with an employer. A resume screams that you are looking for a job and is usually the death knell for the letter and your chances. So, be bold and send the letter without the resume.

Specifics

The enclosure notation can be written several ways. All are acceptable ways to alert the recipient that additional material is enclosed.

- Enclosure
- Encl.
- Enc.
- Appendix A
- Annex B

You can either identify the nature of the enclosure by name or indicate how many pieces are enclosed.

- *Enclosure: Article by I. M. Smith*
- *Encl. (2)*
- *Enc. (3)*

If you identify each piece by name, each item receives its own line, with no spaces between lines.

- *Enclosure: Resume*
- *Enclosure: Article by Joe Smith, ABC Times, December 11, 2001*
- *Enclosure: Certificate of Completion – Marketing Seminar*

If you are copying the letters to others, you will place the copy notation below the enclosure line(s). This allows the recipient of the letter to know who else is receiving a copy. Put each person's name on a separate line.

- *cc: Dr. Joe Black*
  Ms. Jane Smith

Do This . . .

- Include all documents mentioned in your letter. Mention everything you want to send in the body of your letter. If you do not, the reader might wonder why the document is enclosed.

- Include only documents that provide some added value and are relevant to your candidacy. If you are in doubt about the value of a document, do not enclose it initially. You may take it with you to a meeting and decide then if you want to share it with the employer.

- List all documents you are sending; do not leave any out of your enclosure notations.

Don't Do This . . .

- Send something you have not mentioned and identified in both the letter and enclosure notation.

- Forget to send something you mentioned in your letter and enclosure notation.

- Include your resume for an unsolicited approach.

- Send materials that are of poor quality. If you can't reproduce the document you want to send so it is easily read, do not include it.

- List five documents enclosed in the letter and then send only four (or six).

- Send too many documents and attachments with your letter. It will overwhelm the reader.

- Use different enclosure notations in one letter.

Examples of Mistakes to Avoid With Enclosures

Failure to List Items Enclosed:

Enclosure

Being Vague:

Enc: All sorts
Enc: See above

Including Too Many:

Enclosures (15)

Using Different Enclosure Notations in One Letter:

Encl: Resume
Enclosure: Article from ABC Times, December 1, 2001
Enc.: Certificate of Completion

Examples of How to Indicate Enclosures

- *Enc: Appendix A: Resume*
      Appendix B: Photograph of Widget
- *Enclosure: Certificate*
- *Enclosure: Patent of Genealogy*
- *Enclosure: Clipping, "Rescue in Open Sea", The ABC Times, October 11, 2001*
- *Encl. (3)*

Chapter 20

Step 12: The Postscript

Location in the Letter

This item is located at the end of the letter and should be the final line or two.

Align with the left margin.

John Smith
6 Hope Street
Anytown, CA 55555
555-123-4567

January 1, 20XX

Ms. Sue Jones
Production Manager
ABC Company
1234 First Street
Anytown, CA 55555

Dear Ms. Jones:

Your company has developed a unique safety device for wheelchairs that has only been copied by two competitors up to this time.

I completed my studies as a mechanical technician at the ABC College last fall and have always been involved with concerns dealing with people who have physical limitations. I am currently active in a non-profit organization, which concentrates on access availability for wheelchairs.

I have already had the opportunity to work on two projects while in college:

- Marketing: developed 17 technical brochures for a packaging company with $15 million in sales per year;
- Productivity: improved an assembly line for high tech products, resulting in a 17% growth in efficiency in one year.

I would welcome a call from you to set up a meeting. I can be reached at 555-123-4567.

Sincerely,

John Smith

John Smith

Enclosures (3)

P.S. I would like to dedicate at least 30% of my time to commercial development.

Reason and Purpose

A postscript is used for impact to express some thought of importance that has deliberately been withheld from the body of the letter, or to add something you have forgotten to say – an afterthought. In the case of a cover letter, it should only be used for its impact value. If you forget to say something, go back and revise your letter before sending!

It is a short message and should be used with care. It is used as one final attempt to grab the reader's attention in a positive way.

Studies have shown that a postscript has reading power seven times stronger than the rest of the letter! That's a lot of power, so if you use it, be sure it adds something significant.

Degree of Difficulty

This item can be difficult to write so that it accomplishes what you want. Additionally, it is short, so you cannot waste words trying to find the right thing to say. It must be punchy, succinct, and compelling.

Importance in the Letter

The postscript is certainly not mandatory for any letter, and should only be used on rare occasions in a cover letter. You must be certain that its impact will be positive before attempting it.

Specifics

A postscript is usually short and consists of one or two lines only. Current convention uses only the initials P.S., with a period after each letter.

Do This . . .

- Use it only to mention information that is not contained in the body of the letter.

- Make it short and to the point.

- Make sure it is relevant and necessary.

- In some cases, it is better to handwrite the P.S. than to type it. This will make it stand out. If you choose this option, make sure your handwriting is legible and attractive. Do not make the reader struggle to decipher what you have written. Remember that handwriting is a very personal thing and can convey more than the words written, so consider this carefully.

Don't Do This . . .

- Use it to say something you have already said. It is not for emphasis, but rather for impact.
- Write anything that does not directly support your approach.
- Write trivial or unimportant information.
- Use it to refer to your resume.
- Use slang or jargon.

Examples of Mistakes to Avoid With Your Postscript

Repeating Yourself:

> P.S: *I hope that what is said here above will attract your attention.*

Asking for Something That Doesn't Add Impact to the Letter:

> P.S.: *I look forward to your invitation for a meeting.*
>
> P.S.: *I remain at your entire disposal for any additional information you may require.*

Referring to a Resume:

> P.S. *As you can see from my resume, I am well qualified for this job.*

Examples of Language to Use for Your Postscript

- P.S.: *I will be moving to your area in the very near future and will offer these new services to your industry.*
- P.S.: *I would like to dedicate at least 30% of my time to commercial development.*
- P.S. *My fluency in Italian and Spanish may be just what you need as you expand into European markets.*
- P.S. *Two of the web sites I designed have just won industry awards for content and format.*

3 Section Three

The Nuts and Bolts

Chapter **21**
Design and Layout

Design

A cover letter should follow the design of a standard business letter. The purpose of the letter is to convey information to an employer in such a way that they might like to know more about you and will call you for a meeting. You are not auditioning for some creative graphic award; don't use zany styles to set your letter apart from others. This is not the time to step outside the mainstream in design. In terms of design, standard will help more than originality – save the originality for the content.

> Standard design will help more than originality. Save the originality for the content.

Use either Full Block style, where all elements of the letter are aligned to the left margin, or a Modified Block style, where the sender's address, date, complimentary closing, signature, and typed name are aligned down the middle of the page. All other elements of the letters are aligned to the left. Either style is fine.

Layout

The layout of the letter should be one page with no more than five paragraphs. It is fine to use a mirror style, bullets, or a matrix design of some kind to make your text stand out. Do not double-space between paragraphs.

Margins

Margins are traditionally set at 1 inch on the four sides of the document. This leaves some "white space," to make reading easier and doesn't overwhelm the reader with text.

In some cases when your letter is shorter, you may to set the margins at either $1^{1/4}$ or even $1^{1/2}$ inches, if by doing so the letter is still one page in length.

In rare cases, you may find by setting the margins at $^{3/4}$ of an inch, you can get just enough room to keep your letter to one page in length. Never set the margins less than this, however. If you must change things to keep your letter to one page, it is better to either edit out some text or remove spaces between lines, if you have any extras. When these changes don't work, you will have to use a second page. It is better to have two pages than to eliminate important information. Don't use the occasion of moving to two pages, however, as license to fill up the entire second page with more text.

Ink Color

Print your letter using black ink. Do not use colors – no red, green, orange, or purple ever! You may sign your letter in blue ink so it will stand out a bit from the printed page, or you can use black. No colored inks should be used for writing your signature either.

Length of the Letter

> The letter is meant to outline why you are writing – not to list every achievement you've ever had.

It is recommended that you keep your letter to a single page. If you cannot do that without compromising the quality of your letter, you may go to two pages. Under no circumstances should your letter be longer than two pages. You will lose your reader's good will!

Your letter is meant to briefly outline why you are writing and what you can offer to the employer. It is not the place for you to list every achievement you've ever had, nor explain problems in your past.

If you use two pages, you must make a notation on the top of your second page that references the letter. This way, if the pages become separated, the reader will know where the second page belongs. Do not use letterhead for your second page. If you carry over to a second page, bring your last paragraph so you don't just have your signature block on this page.

To reference the second page of the letter, type the name of the recipient, the page number, and the date. This will be left flush to the margin as indicated in this example.

Recipient's Name
Page Two
Date

It is also acceptable to place this information across the top of the page if you prefer that style, as shown in the example below.

Recipient's Name　　　*Page Two*　　　*Date*

You may add the RE: line if you have used one, but only if it is short.

Typed or Written in Longhand

In most cases, you should type your letter to maintain a professional appearance. When you do this, you have four advantages:

- It is legible and the reader will not struggle to understand it.
- It looks professional.
- You can highlight important words with the use of the **bold** function.
- You can easily modify or edit your letter without starting over if you want to make changes.

In very rare cases, a letter may be handwritten. It will make your letter stand out and can create a personal feeling. If you do this, use only black ink and keep your letter brief. Remember that handwritten letters may be subject to a graphology analysis without your awareness or permission, which could be used to screen you out, however unscientific or unreliable this may be. We recommend sending a typed letter.

Typeface/Font and Size

There are hundreds and thousands of choices now, but stick to either a serif (meaning with little lines on the edges of the letters) that help with the recognition of characters and are great for longer text because the reader's eye can focus more easily. Times or Times New Roman are popular serif fonts. This paragraph uses a Times serif font.

A sans serif font (meaning without those little lines) is usually considered more elegant and simple to read. Popular sans serif fonts are Arial, Helvetica, and Lucida Grande. This paragraph uses an Arial sans serif font.

Stick with only one font, especially in a document as short as a letter. It is not a good idea to mix fonts, such as serif with sans serif for short documents, or use more than one font. If you want to highlight something, you can use either **bold** or *italics*. The most common font size for standard letters and resumes is 12 point. It is acceptable to use 11, 13, and even 14, but do not use anything smaller or larger than these.

This is okay (sometimes) – 11 point

This is okay – 12 point and most common

This is okay – 13 point

This is okay (rarely) – 14 pt.

This is not okay – 10 point

This is not okay – 15 point

Chapter 22
Paper and Envelope

Paper

A standard business size ($8^{1/2}$ x 11) paper should be used for letters and resumes. This is often called "A" (letter) size.

Color

Paper color doesn't really matter very much, if you don't stray out of bounds of reasonable choices. Paper is usually white, but off-white, ecru, ivory, light beige, gray, or light blue are also acceptable. You probably aren't going to be kicked out of the running if your paper is a light goldenrod color. By the same token, don't think that by choosing some unusual color like seaweed green, you'll have an advantage and stand out from the rest of the stack causing the reader to grab your letter first.

> Paper color doesn't matter very much, if you don't stray out of bounds.

If you are sending a resume with your letter, be sure that the paper is the same for both documents. Don't send a resume on blue paper with a letter on gray paper. Match your paper and envelopes for regular mail. When using letterhead, make sure your accompanying papers (2nd sheet, resume, and envelope) match.

Do not use "stationary" type paper with pre-printed designs. It doesn't look professional.

Don't use paper with background designs, like those with a marbled effect or dots. This will make it unreadable if the letter is faxed or scanned, as the fax/scanner won't be able to differentiate the text from the background design. Dark-colored papers don't copy or fax well either.

Weight

The weight of a paper is measured in pounds based on a ream of 500 sheets cut to a standard size. That equates, for a paper considered to have a 20 lb. weight, to five pounds per ream.

Paper weights should run from 20 lb. to 24 lb. for your correspondence; 28 lb. paper is also acceptable in some cases. Cover stock at 60 lbs. is too heavy for letters. It will not easily go through printers or fax machines.

If you know your letter or resume will be scanned, use 20 lb. paper to be sure that the paper will work with most common scanners used by businesses. Do not use staples to attach resumes or other documents for correspondence that might be scanned or faxed. It is better to use a paper clip.

Texture

There are three different kinds of good quality paper that can be used for your letters and resumes.

1. **Cotton paper** is paper made from durable cotton fibers. It is strong and holds up well under frequent handling. The higher the cotton content in paper the better its quality – sometimes called "rag" content. "Bond" is another term for high cotton fiber paper, originating after World War II when war bonds were printed on cotton fiber paper. Cotton is the most commonly used paper for letters and resumes. Use at least a 25% cotton fiber content paper.

2. **Laid paper** is paper with a textured finish usually consisting of a horizontal pattern and a vertical pattern known as "chain lines." During the manufacturing process, the pattern is pressed into the paper to create the texture. Laid papers are considered elegant and project a sophisticated image, but have a slightly coarser feel to them. The drawbacks with laid paper are that it doesn't always hold ink from lesser quality printers and is sometimes hard to fold.

3. **Linen paper** is paper with a textured finish applied by an embossing process done after the paper has been manufactured. It looks and feels like linen fabric.

Coated paper, while nice for a magazine or brochure, isn't recommended for your correspondence.

A watermark is an image that is applied to the paper during manufacturing which many people feel gives a sense of prestige to the paper. A watermark is visible from the front and the back of the paper when held up to light. The image cannot be copied or scanned and was originally placed on paper to discourage counterfeiting, although today it is used as a sign of a good quality paper.

Envelope

Size

In most cases, a standard commercial style envelope will be used to mail your letter. When possible your envelopes should match your paper. Do not use brightly colored envelopes or those with fancy designs for this purpose.

U.S. envelopes are known as Standard sizes, or #10 business envelopes, which are $4^{1/8}$ x $9^{1/2}$. ISO is the metric system used in Europe and many other parts of the world to categorize envelopes and uses the C series that was designed to accommodate the ISO "A" paper sizes. ISO is called C5 and is similar in size to the #10 business envelope.

The Commercial style (below) is the most popular envelope for business correspondence. It requires that you fold your document into three sections.

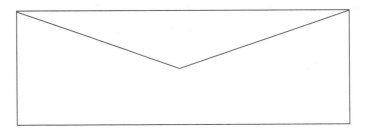

You may wish to use a Catalog style (below) envelope for mailing your letter and resume and/or other documents if you do not wish to fold them. While it's more cumbersome and will cost more for postage, your documents will arrive intact and without creases. The most common size for this is 9 x 12.

Return Address

Make sure your return address is on the envelope. You may place it on the back flap on your envelope or in the left top corner. If possible, use a computer to print this information so it looks more professional, or use preprinted envelopes that match your letterhead. If that isn't possible, neatly print your information or use a label. Do not use big, frilly, or goofy labels. White is best for labels.

Postage

Make sure you have the correct amount of postage on the envelope – a large envelope will require extra postage. There is nothing worse than sending off your letter, after all the effort and time you've put into it, believing it has reached the recipient, only to have it returned to you five days later for insufficient postage. Worst yet, is to have made the recipient pay the missing postage.

In some rare cases when sending your letter by traditional mail, you may want to include a self-addressed stamped envelope to increase the chances of receiving a response from the recipient. In most cases, however, this will not be necessary.

Chapter *Delivery* **23**

Y ou've done the hard work of researching, writing, and proofing your letter. Now the $64,000 question! How to you deliver your letter to the person you wish to reach?

You have four basic choices. You can:

- Personally deliver it to the person/company
- Send it by special courier (UPS, FedEx, DHL)
- Mail it using the United States Postal Service (now lovingly referred to as snail mail)
- Email it

Each of these four methods has advantages and disadvantages.

If you personally deliver it to the person/company

This is clearly the most time-consuming and least practical method to use and consequently least used option. The key advantage is that you might just be lucky enough to run into the person you've written to and spend a few unscheduled minutes with them. If not an actual interview, it might be enough time for them to become interested in you and then call you back for an "official" interview. Assuming you are delivering your letter locally, you can get the letter there fast when pushed for time (if the deadline to apply is TODAY). If you choose this method, be prepared when you go, by dressing well and knowing what you want to say if you run into the recipient. If you have someone else drop it off for you, there is no risk!

If you send your letter by special courier (UPS, FedEx, DHL)

The main drawback to this option is it will cost you! If you're sending out a lot of letters, this method might become prohibitive. The advantage is you know your letter will be delivered in one or two days – whatever time you've selected – and it will stand out from the rest of the group by its larger envelope and the fact the employer knows you spent good money to send it. It will probably get to the place you want it to go, as most folks won't throw away a special delivery letter without checking it out first.

If you mail your letter using the United States Postal Service – now lovingly referred to as snail mail

This is the most traditional and often used method for mailing a tangible letter. It's cheap – almost everyone can afford the stamp needed. It's easy to do; you put your letter out for the mailperson or drop it in a post box.

The drawback is, of course, that your letter arrives looking just like the other 200 letters arriving on the same day. Your letter will not stand out in any way. You may choose to mark it "Personal and Confidential" but that doesn't seem to carry much weight these days with most folks. It's an easy assumption – if it looks like a letter of application, it is a letter of application – and most people don't consider that personal anymore.

If you email it

Obviously, this is the quickest, easiest, and now most commonly used method. It's fast – only one second from hitting the Send button until delivery – and no paper is involved. What could be easier than that? It's cheap – no stamp is needed and there's no driving to the post office or FedEx center. The problem with email is there is no paper involved, unless the recipient decides to print it out, so there is no paper record of your communication. It is easy to ignore it, open it and close it in four seconds, when it doesn't catch the interest of the reader, or simply delete it to move it out of the already overloaded inbox. The Delete key is always within reach and easy to push! It's the preferred key of screeners!

The Great Debate of Email vs. Regular Mail

There's debate among professionals in the field of career assistance about which is a better way to go when sending in your letter and/or resume. Some employers like email; some don't. It's hard to know which employers are which, however, if you don't ask them up front. There are articles written all the time debating the pros and cons of each method. There aren't any real statistical studies to point to that say definitively which is the better method.

What don't employers like about email? Well, for one, they are bombarded with hundreds of messages a day. Opening up the inbox becomes a frightening event! They know it is going to take a lot of time to open each message, see if it's worth reading, and if it is, read it and perhaps respond, or forward to someone else who should have been the recipient of the message in the first place (if you are lucky).

For another, some job hunters forget that email is real communication and deserves all the niceties and practical etiquette of a regular letter. It's not the time for sloppy writing, missed salutations and closings, or running on and on, rationalizing that since it isn't printed out it doesn't matter if the letter goes on for 5,000 words.

What do employers like about email? It's what we all like about email – it's fast and immediate. If an employer likes what you've sent, they can respond very fast and impersonally – no time wasted searching around for a number. No time spent on the phone trying to reach you. No cost to hit that reply button. They can let you know they are interested and outline the next step, or if they are the polite type, they can say "no thanks" easily, in a couple of sentences. If they don't like it, they can delete the file or let it fall off the edge of the cyber world, without ever having to give it another thought.

They also like that their file cabinet is only as big as a hard drive and that's small these days! No paper to mess with or file or lose!

The other tremendous advantage of email is that it reduces the size of the world. You can be in Beijing, China, or across the hall from the person receiving the email, and each of these communications are as close and intimate as the other. It is seamless and brings any and every part of the world to any doorstep, or inbox in this case. As far as the written word is concerned, email is a gift to all of us in bringing us closer.

Since email seems to be pretty well accepted and even the preferred method of communicating by some, you are probably safe to send your letter this way. If you have doubts, you can either:

- Call the company and ask them outright their preferred method of delivery.
- Send your letter, both by email and by snail mail, covering the bases.

Just as employers have preferences, so do we. Unless an employer specifically requests an email response, we think you do yourself a greater service by sending your letter by regular mail. There is then some tangible proof of your efforts and chances are better that someone will actually open your envelope. This will increase the possibility that your letter may actually be read. It may not be provable, but if someone takes the time to open your letter, they will probably give it at least a moment or two, to see what you have written.

If you do use email, be sure to:

- Attach files if you say you are sending something else along with the letter. Be sure you have referenced this in the body of your letter.

- Use a PDF file, rather than a document created in an application, so that the recipient can open it – in many cases, the recipient won't be able to open documents created in programs they do not have or their server won't let through. A PDF file doesn't allow the recipient the opportunity to see what corrections you've made to your documents either, as some applications do.

- Observe social etiquette and include pleasantries and normal and expected salutations and closings.

- Print out your letter prior to sending, so you will have a copy for your files and can double-check how it looks when printed out. The recipient may print it out.

- Use the subject line, so the recipient will know at a glance why you are writing and not dismiss the email as spam.

- Spell-check, proof, spell-check and proof again. DO NOT send a letter with ANY mistakes.

Chapter *Writing Style* 24

I f you have questions about what writing style to adopt, it is best to be direct. Use the least amount of words to convey what you want to say. Measure each word for its impact and importance, and if it isn't necessary, get rid of it. While **content** is what's most important, **brevity** is how to get your letter read. If what you say isn't germane or interesting, however, it won't matter if your letter is short. On the other hand if your letter goes on and on, a reader will be defeated before they ever begin.

> While content is what's most important, brevity is how to get your letter read.

Remember, the goal of your letter is to get a meeting. Use every tactic you can to your advantage to reach this goal. You are not trying to win a literary prize in this instance, so stay focused on your end goal. Business people, who read these letters, aren't looking for literary prose; they want to get to the bottom line fast. They want to know, "What's in it for me?"

Try writing as if you were speaking to another person and had only three minutes to tell them your story. This will help you eliminate extraneous information that doesn't add to your case. Remember the rule you learned in grammar school:

> **Sentence** = subject + verb + object

It will help you as you compose your letter.

If you have difficulties with spelling and grammar, most word-proccessing programs include spelling and grammar checking capabilities. If you are creating your letter in MS Word application, you can do the following to check the reading level of your document (using the Word X version):

1. On the Word menu, click **Preferences**, and then click **Spelling and Grammar**.

2. Select the **Check Grammar With Spelling** check box.

3. Select the **Show Readability** statistics check box, and then click OK.

4. On the Tools menu, click **Spelling and Grammar** to use on each document.

Check your manual or the help menu if you use a different version of Word to see how you can enable the Readability Index. When Word finishes checking spelling and grammar, it displays information about the reading level of the document. Each readability score bases its rating on the average number of syllables per word and words per sentence.

Sentence Length

The "Flesch Reading Ease" score rates text on a 100-point scale; the higher the score, the easier it is to understand the document. For most standard letters you should aim for a score of approximately 60 to 70. The "Flesch-Kincaid Grade Level" score rates text on a U.S. grade-school level. For example, a score of 8.0 means that an eighth grader can understand the document. For most standard letters, aim for a score of approximately 7.0 to 8.0.

> Let's try this experiment and see what you think the value of a sentence that goes on and on might have on an employer who is trying to read through 200 resumes and letters in one afternoon and can't really make up their mind about which candidates to call in for interviews because so many of the letters and resumes seem to represent candidates who could probably do the job just fine but they have to find some way to narrow down the pool of applicants in order to make the job manageable.

That's a 93-word sentence. Too long?
The grade level score on this one sentence is 12.0.

> Let's try this experiment. And see what you think the value of a sentence. That goes on and on might have. On an employer who is trying to read through 200 resumes. And letters in one afternoon. And can't really make up their mind. Which ones to call in for interviews. Because so many of the letters and resumes represent candidates. Who could probably do the job just fine. But they have to find some way to narrow down. The pool of applicants in order to make the job manageable.

11 Sentences – too choppy?
The grade level score on these fragmented sentences is 3.8.

Both examples are equally awful!

Find a Balance

Find a balance in your writing. Keep paragraphs short. Keep the length at five to seven lines. Vary your sentences. Mix longer ones with shorter ones and occasionally use a sentence fragment if you wish. You can begin one or two sentences with the conjunctions "and," "but," or "because." But don't do it too often!

To have a greater impact, your sentences need to have the following five characteristics:

1. **Clarity:** Assume your reader is not familiar with your subject matter, and write as if explaining it to them (not in a condescending way but assuming they have little familiarity with the topic).

2. **Active Voice:** Use an active voice, rather than a passive one.

    Say: *7 seminars were presented to alumni.*
    Don't Say: *Alumni were presented with 7 seminars.*

3. **Convincing:** The beginning of the sentence has the most impact, so start off strong. For example, if you want to put the emphasis on "absenteeism":

    Say: *The absenteeism rate of blue-collar worker has decreased by...*
    Don't Say: *The blue-collar workers have had an absenteeism rate that has decreased by...*

4. **Brevity:** Try to keep your sentences short, using 12-14 words only.

    - Do not exceed 20 words.
    - Carefully consider what you want to say and do not stray from the main points.
    - Eliminate the "background noise"! In other words, don't put in every detail and clutter up your main points.
    - Sequence your ideas.
    - Stick with essentials.
    - Focus on your reader and think how your letter comes across to them.
    - Use keywords and build your sentences around them.
    - Use supporting sentences sparingly.

5. **Positive:** Keep your tone positive. Do not talk in the negative.

    Say: *The tables were clean and empty.*
    Don't Say: *There were no papers or documents on the tables.*

Do not say	Better to say
3% failed	97% succeeded
I have never made such…	I always wanted to …
I was not responsible for…	I took the initiative to…
Negative…	Positive…

Adopt an assertive style and do not hesitate or show a lack of self-confidence.

Do not say	Better to say
It is possible…	Facts demonstrate that…
I consider…	I have decided …
I am looking for…	I am interested…I am attracted by…
I do not know…	I have to reflect on it…
I wish…	I have decided that…

Use expressions that show initiative.

Do not say	Better to say
I had to…	I contributed…
I helped…	They selected me for…
I was obliged to…	I was chosen for…
They asked me to…	I was chosen for…
They asked me to…	I succeeded in…
They asked me to…	The company gave me the responsibility…
They asked me to…	The company entrusted me to…
They asked me to…	I took the initiative of…
They gave me…	I decided to…
They placed me in…	I took the initiative to set up…
They placed me in…	They trusted me to…
They placed me in…	I was invited to…

Stay away from words of a "suicidal" nature.

I was stuck by…
I had to…
I was hired for…
I have had to…

I do not have much experience but...
I do not know whether...
I am afraid of being too old...
I tried hard to...
I do not know if...
They asked me to...
They imposed on me the job of...

Some Specific Tips

Avoid overusing "I" or "I have"

The overuse of "I" and "I have" at the beginning of sentences can be overcome by substituting:

- With the help of...
- By favoring...
- By using...
- Thanks to...
- The XYZ Company asked me to...
- We...
- Without the help of...
- As proof of this...
- As the person in charge of..., I

It is still better yet to change "I have" into "you want" – and speak to your reader's needs. If every paragraph in your letter begins with the word "I," you have missed the boat. Make sure that is not the case with your letters.

Use numbers for your figures – do not spell out numbers

The figures you use are not intended to impress your reader so much as to give credibility or authenticity to the action you mention. Show the reader that you know how to measure efficiency and the impact of your work with figures. Use absolute values.

Do not say	Better to say
Four	4
Thirteen	13
Seventy-two	72

Do not use an abbreviation for amounts of money, such as M, m, or K. You may use the symbols for currencies, however, such as €, £, $, CHF, Sfr, CN, $, and so forth.

Do not say	Better to say
Five million	5 million
$8 M	$8 million
2.5 M	$2.5 million
50K	$50,000

Avoid estimations

It is best to use numbers to quantify your statements.

Do not say	Better to say
Some...	More than 10...
Many...	More than 20...
More or less...	Approximately 12

Watch the words you use

Watch your vocabulary! Stay away from technical terms, abbreviations, and other initials. Think of your reader. Use words that are:

- **Clear:** Don't overuse sophisticated terms and ideas. Translate foreign words using brackets { } or [ ].

- **Precise:** Replace vague words with concrete terms. Avoid vague statements, and use specifics.

- **Simple:** Be as brief as possible and substitute convoluted words for straightforward words. Use examples.

"Effectively" and "efficiently" are extremely overused. Use an example instead that states in concrete terms what was "efficient" or "effective." In other words, **how** you were efficient and effective – write that instead!

Use appropriate expressions

Center around

Avoid using "center around." The correct usage is "center on" or "center in."

Use e.g. and i.e. correctly

These are Latin abbreviations. E.g. means "for example" and i.e. means "that is." It is better to write these expressions out if space permits than to abbreviate them, in case your reader is not familiar with the terms.

- For example, I used 20 different designs on my web sites in the last 5 months.
- I saw the trend in women's clothes moving towards more fluid skirts, that is, skirts with many ruffles and layers.

Give credit to others

If the results you achieved were accomplished with others, say it simply. Be sure to give others credit when it is due.

Be sensitive to confidential information

Before you publish figures or rates, check with your former employer(s) to make sure this is acceptable. Thank them with a letter confirming the authorization that was given to you verbally.

Know your audience

When citing illustrations and achievements, use language the recipient will understand and that fits with their experience.

For example, do not say that you "increased a fleet of vehicles from 240 to 1,800" if the company which you approach is only at a level of 15 units!

Do not quote "a 55 % growth rate per year" to an organization that is growing at the rate of 7% a year.

Add some mystery to the mix

Include some mystery that may pique the reader's interest.

For example:

- *by 3 simple methods applicable to your company*
- *by a methodology used in Canada*
- *by a method which no company in your field has yet tried*
- *by a simple method*
- *by a technique which few people know about*
- *by a method of unsurpassed speed*
- *by a particular method*
- *in a very simple way*
- *by an approach rarely used as a negotiation technique*

Proofread your letter

Proofread your letter. Run spell-check. Proofread again. Always use a dictionary if you have any doubt about the spelling of a word.

Ask two or three friends to read your letter for content and proofreading. Make corrections One spelling mistake can detract or destroy an otherwise outstanding letter. Spelling and grammar mistakes are hard to forgive because they are unnecessary and show a lack of attention to detail.

To illustrate, see how quickly these sentences make you wonder about the person who wrote them!

- *The apples which we have to store were later sold in 4 months with a margin of 82%.*
- *I was classified the first one of all my team.*
- *The closing of an account was realized within 4 days of its demise.*
- *We resolved this dilemma and managed to keep 77% of our clientelle.*
- *We overtook the problem by allowing the employees to eat lunch with their children in the cafateria.*

Follow punctuation rules

Use basic rules of punctuation. If you are in doubt about punctuation rules, refer to one of many online sources of information or buy a book on punctuation, such as *Eats, Shoots & Leaves: The Zero Tolerance Approach to Punctuation*, by Lynne Truss, Gotham (April, 2004).

Emphasize with boldface or italics

Boldface and *italics* can add to your letter by drawing the reader's eye to certain words or sections. They should be used only occasionally, as overuse dilutes their effectiveness. Underlining words makes them harder to read due to the line's closeness to actual text, so be careful with this effect. If you use the boldface option to emphasize text, do it no more than 3 to 7 times on a page.

Be careful using adjectives and adverbs

Adjectives and adverbs weaken your letter. If you think you are helping your case to say you are, "competent, motivated, reliable, and enthusiastic," think again. Let your achievements and the corresponding results speak for you. The reader can then decide if you are "competent, motivated, reliable, and enthusiastic"! Replace adjectives and adverbs by data, percentages, ratios, and facts.

Do not say	Better to say
Lightning speed	Less than 6 months
Remarkable	127%
Important	More than 1,200
A sharp increase	An increase of 24%
A large number of shops	182 shops
Large inventories	An inventory of 8 million
Very strong rate	17% rate
Numerous customers	127 customers
Big success	1,200 guests

Using abbreviations and initials

Do not use abbreviations, period. There is no need and the reader may not know what you mean. Use initials only when it is the commonly accepted way to say something.

For example:

- J.R. Nabisco Company
- SBC Global
- I. M. Pei
- RE:
- Encl:
- P.S.

From Confused and Frustrated Job Hunter
to Successfully Employed!

We believe if you've followed the advice and recommendations in this book and done your homework, you will have placed yourself ahead of most job hunters in the market. We know that writing effective cover letters can make a difference in your job hunting efforts, because thousands of people who have invested the time and energy to do it right have told us so. We hope you will count yourself in that number the next time you look for a job.

Appendix A
Writing Your
Achievement Paragraphs

Form 1
Building Your Achievement Paragraphs

The following four forms can help you write achievement paragraphs. Copy them and fill out for each achievement. If you need more space for any one item, use a separate sheet of paper. The pages following Form 1 contain a checklist titled "7 Ways to Quantify Achievements," which can help you fill out the Results section below.

Name of Job/Function: _____

    A. Tasks Involved:

        _____
        _____
        _____

    B. Means (what did you use to do it?)

        _____
        _____
        _____

    C. Results (quantified)

        1.   Increase:

            _____
            _____
            _____

        2.   Decrease:

            _____
            _____
            _____

        3.   Suppression–Eradicate–Eliminate

            _____
            _____
            _____

        4.   Bypass

            _____
            _____
            _____

        5.   Repetition–Systemization–Duplication

            _____
            _____
            _____

        6.   Distinction

            _____
            _____
            _____

        7.   Creation–Invention–Conception

            _____
            _____
            _____

7 Ways to Quantify Achievements

Achievements can be quantified in at least seven different ways. The following list shows many ways to best show how your results can be measured. Look through the list to see which categories apply to each of your achievements. Be sure to use real numbers, percentages, or other measurable information when possible to complete the quantification.

---

1. Increase In

Quantified Examples

- ❑ Contacts
- ❑ Customers
- ❑ Distributors
- ❑ Efficiency
- ❑ Length of meetings
- ❑ Loading
- ❑ Markets/Segments/Niches
- ❑ Penetration
- ❑ People approached/trained
- ❑ People welcomed
- ❑ Reference checks
- ❑ Production capacity
- ❑ Productivity
- ❑ Profitability/Gross margin/ Cash flow
- ❑ Referral
- ❑ Repeat rate
- ❑ Sales/Turnover
- ❑ Satisfaction
- ❑ Selling price
- ❑ Services
- ❑ Speed reporting
- ❑ Success
- ❑ Surface/Area/Territory
- ❑ Telephone calls
- ❑ Visits/Calls
- ❑ Workshops/Conferences/Events

2. Decrease Of

Quantified Examples

- ❏ Absenteeism
- ❏ Accidents
- ❏ Bad debts
- ❏ Breakage
- ❏ Budget variation
- ❏ Contracts
- ❏ Costs
- ❏ Delays
- ❏ Delinquent payers
- ❏ Density
- ❏ Discounts
- ❏ Equipment/People used
- ❏ Failures
- ❏ Garbage
- ❏ Goods in process
- ❏ Invoice preparation time
- ❏ Invoicing delay
- ❏ Litigation
- ❏ Losses
- ❏ Meetings/Visits/Interviews
- ❏ No other products in stock
- ❏ Packages
- ❏ Paper
- ❏ Personnel
- ❏ Personnel turnover
- ❏ Pollution
- ❏ Reports/Correspondence
- ❏ Subcontracts
- ❏ Suppliers
- ❏ Thefts
- ❏ Unproductive time
- ❏ Unsold goods

3. Suppression Of   Quantified Examples

- ❑ Accidents   _____
- ❑ Claims   _____
- ❑ Companies/Subsidiaries   _____
- ❑ Discounts   _____
- ❑ Documents/Correspondence   _____
- ❑ Errors   _____
- ❑ Inventories   _____
- ❑ Jobs   _____
- ❑ Losses   _____
- ❑ Meetings   _____
- ❑ Methods (antiquated)   _____
- ❑ Mistakes   _____
- ❑ Nuisances   _____
- ❑ Pirating   _____
- ❑ Premiums   _____
- ❑ Products (loss centers)   _____
- ❑ Promotional actions (not targeted)   _____
- ❑ Resistance   _____
- ❑ Returns   _____
- ❑ Risks   _____
- ❑ Taxes   _____
- ❑ Thefts   _____
- ❑ Unnecessary business lunches   _____
- ❑ Visits   _____

4. Bypass   Quantified Examples

- ❑ Accidents   _____
- ❑ Communication breakdown   _____
- ❑ Conflicts   _____
- ❑ Costs   _____
- ❑ Failures   _____
- ❑ Fraud   _____
- ❑ Insurance premium increases   _____
- ❑ Invasion from competition   _____
- ❑ Late penalties   _____

- ❑ Loss of customers/orders   _____
- ❑ Orders canceled   _____
- ❑ Out of stock   _____
- ❑ Personnel turnover   _____
- ❑ Planning errors   _____
- ❑ Provisions on the balance sheet   _____
- ❑ Recruitment   _____
- ❑ Returns   _____
- ❑ Suppliers price increase   _____
- ❑ Thefts   _____
- ❑ Unannounced visitors   _____
- ❑ Unprofitable investments   _____

5. Repetition   **Quantified Examples**

- ❑ Budgets   _____
- ❑ Classifying systems   _____
- ❑ Compensation/reparation   _____
- ❑ Documents   _____
- ❑ Exhibitions   _____
- ❑ Job descriptions   _____
- ❑ Maintenance   _____
- ❑ Newsletters/Bulletins   _____
- ❑ Open door days   _____
- ❑ Procedures (accounting, recruitment)   _____
- ❑ Promotions   _____
- ❑ Repeat business   _____
- ❑ Surveys/Studies   _____
- ❑ Training events   _____
- ❑ Visits   _____
- ❑ Ways to handle cases   _____

6. Distinction   **Quantified Examples**

- ❑ Awards/Congratulations   _____
- ❑ Mentions in the press   _____
- ❑ Promotions   _____

❑   Proposals _____

❑   Ranking in media _____

❑   Selection for experimental projects _____

❑   Surveys _____

❑   Thank you calls/Letters _____

_____

7. Creation Of: **Quantified Examples**

❑   Advertising campaigns _____

❑   Booth _____

❑   Classifying concepts _____

❑   Computerization _____

❑   Concepts _____

❑   Departments/Sub-companies _____

❑   Documents _____

❑   Feedback procedures _____

❑   Files (customers, suppliers) _____

❑   Flyers/Brochures _____

❑   Image (product, company) _____

❑   Information systems _____

❑   Measuring tools _____

❑   Models _____

❑   Procedures _____

❑   Products/Services _____

❑   Promotional tools/methods _____

❑   Prototypes _____

❑   Quality control _____

❑   Reporting procedures _____

❑   Security/protection systems _____

❑   Standard letters/Mail _____

❑   Tasks/Missions _____

❑   Training modules _____

_____

Form 2
Detailing Your Achievement

The following two forms can be used to refine and narrow down all the information needed for an achievement statement/paragraph.

1. Describe an achievement, task, or issue that you have carried out and enjoyed.
    _____
    _____
    _____

2. Where did it take place? (Name of employer, place?)
    _____
    _____
    _____

3. What were your job titles and responsibilities?
    _____
    _____
    _____

4. Did you do it by yourself or in a group? If in a group, with whom?
    _____
    _____
    _____

5. Mention one thing that made your achievement difficult.
    _____
    _____
    _____

6. How did you overcome the difficulty?
    _____
    _____
    _____

7. Did you do it well? What tangible result or proof can you show that you achieved your goal?
    _____
    _____
    _____

Form 3
Write Up Your Achievement

1st Version

I have . . . (verb/skill)	[ ]	Result (quantified)	[ ]

2nd Version

Result
I managed to . . . When I completed my task/mission . . .
_____
_____

Difficult condition
It was difficult since . . .
_____
_____

Alone/in group
I was . . .
_____
_____

Mystery
To achieve this task/mission, I . . .
_____
_____

Bridge to prospective employer
I did it in an organization, which like yours . . .
_____
_____

Key idea or point of achievement

[ ]

3rd Version – *Rewrite achievement until it is ready to use in your letter.*

[ ]

[ ]

Form 4
Flash Test: 10 Key Points

Check either the "Modify" box and include your recommendations, or the "Good" box. Re-do each achievement paragraph until all boxes are "Good." Once your achievement statement/paragraph is written, use this flash test to make sure it is complete and ready to be used.

		Modify	Recommendation	Good
1	Tangible and quantified results are mentioned.	❏		❏
2	Achievement described makes sense and is easily understandable.	❏		❏
3	Only one idea or point is developed.	❏		❏
4	There is some mystery and the reader will want to know more.	❏		❏
5	Some key issues are addressed: where, why, when, but not how!	❏		❏
6	Sentences are short – 12 to 15 words.	❏		❏
7	Vocabulary used is one the recipient knows.	❏		❏
8	Sentences and words used are positive.	❏		❏
9	Text runs between 3 to 5 typed lines per achievement.	❏		❏
10	There is very limited use of adjectives or adverbs, and then used only to describe means or numbers involved.	❏		❏

Action Verbs to Help You Get Started

A

Accelerated
Accomplished
Achieved
Acted
Activated
Adapted
Addressed
Adjusted
Administered
Advanced
Advertised
Advised
Advocated
Aided
Allocated
Analyzed
Answered
Applied
Appraised
Approved
Arbitrated
Arranged
Ascertained
Assembled
Assessed
Assigned
Assisted
Attained
Augmented
Authorized
Awarded

B

Balanced
Began
Boosted
Briefed
Budgeted
Built

C

Calculated
Captured
Cataloged
Centralized
Chaired
Charted
Checked
Clarified
Classified
Coached
Collaborated
Collected
Combined
Communicated
Compared
Compiled
Completed
Composed
Computed
Conceived
Conceptualized
Condensed
Conducted
Conferred
Conserved
Consolidated
Constructed
Consulted
Contacted
Continued
Contributed
Controlled
Converted
Conveyed
Convinced
Coordinated
Corresponded
Counseled
Created
Critiqued

Cultivated
Customized

D

Debugged
Decided
Defined
Delegated
Delivered
Demonstrated
Designated
Designed
Detected
Determined
Developed
Devised
Diagnosed
Directed
Discovered
Dispensed
Displayed
Dissected
Distributed
Diverted
Documented
Drafted

E

Earned
Edited
Educated
Effected
Eliminated
Emphasized
Employed
Encouraged
Enforced
Engineered
Enhanced
Enlarged
Enlisted
Ensured

Entertained
Established
Estimated
Evaluated
Examined
Executed
Expanded
Expedited
Experimented
Explained
Explored
Expressed
Extended
Extracted

F

Fabricated
Facilitated
Fashioned
Finalized
Fixed
Focused
Forecasted
Formed
Formulated
Fostered
Found
Fulfilled
Furnished

G

Gained
Gathered
Generated
Governed
Grossed
Guided

H

Handled
Headed
Heightened
Helped
Hired
Honed
Hosted
Hypothesized

I

Identified
Illustrated
Imagined
Implemented
Improved
Improvised
Incorporated
Increased
Indexed
Influenced
Informed
Initiated
Innovated
Inspected
Inspired
Installed
Instituted
Integrated
Interacted
Interpreted
Interviewed
Introduced
Invented
Inventoried
Investigated
Involved
Issued

J

Joined
Judged

K

Kept

L

Launched
Learned
Lectured
Led
Lifted
Listened
Located
Logged

M

Maintained
Managed
Manipulated
Marketed
Maximized
Measured
Mediated
Merged
Mobilized
Modified
Monitored
Motivated

N

Navigated
Negotiated
Netted

O

Observed
Obtained
Opened
Operated
Ordered
Orchestrated
Organized
Originated
Outlined
Overcame
Overhauled
Oversaw

P

Participated
Performed
Persuaded
Photographed
Pinpointed
Piloted
Pioneered
Placed
Planned
Played
Predicted
Prepared

Prescribed
Presented
Presided
Prevented
Printed
Prioritized
Processed
Produced
Programmed
Projected
Promoted
Proofread
Proposed
Protected
Proved
Provided
Publicized
Purchased

Q

Qualified
Questioned

R

Raised
Ran
Rated
Reached
Realized
Reasoned
Received
Recommended
Reconciled
Recorded
Recruited
Reduced
Referred
Regulated
Rehabilitated
Related
Remodeled
Rendered
Reorganized
Repaired
Replaced
Reported

Represented
Researched
Reshaped
Resolved
Responded
Restored
Retrieved
Reviewed
Revised
Revitalized
Routed

S

Saved
Scheduled
Screened
Searched
Secured
Selected
Separated
Served
Shaped
Shared
Simplified
Simulated
Sketched
Sold
Solved
Sorted
Spearheaded
Specialized
Specified
Spoke
Sponsored
Staffed
Standardized
Started
Streamlined
Strengthened
Structured
Studied
Suggested
Summarized
Supervised
Supplied
Supported

Surpassed
Surveyed
Sustained
Synthesized
Systematized

T

Targeted
Taught
Terminated
Tested
Tightened
Totaled
Tracked
Traded
Trained
Transcribed
Transformed
Translated
Transmitted
Traveled
Tutored

U

Uncovered
Undertook
Unified
United
Updated
Upgraded
Used
Utilized

V

Validated
Verbalized
Verified
Vitalized
Volunteered

W

Weighed
Widened
Won
Worked
Wrote

Appendix B

Letter Examples

John Smith
6 Hope Street
Anytown, CA 55555
555-123-4567

January 1, 20XX

Ms. Sue Jones
Production Manager
ABC Company
1234 First Street
Anytown, CA 55555

Dear Ms. Jones:

Your company has developed a unique safety device for wheelchairs that has only been copied by two competitors up to this time. I have thought of two additional ways to improve these wheelchairs that will make copying these safety devices very difficult.

I completed my studies as a mechanical technician at the ABC College last fall and have always been involved with concerns dealing with people who have physical limitations. I am currently active in a non-profit organization, which concentrates on access availability for wheelchairs in high-rise buildings in Anytown.

I have already had the opportunity to work on two projects while in college:

- Marketing: developed 12 technical brochures for a packaging company with $15 million in sales per year;
- Productivity: improved an assembly line for high tech products, resulting in a 17% growth in efficiency in one year.

I would welcome a call from you to set up a meeting. I can be reached at 555-123-4567.

Sincerely,

John Smith

John Smith

COMMENTS: As a recent graduate, the author of this letter has had no formal job in this area, but uses his two internships to show what he has done and how his skills and interests would benefit this employer. He uses results oriented statements, stating facts and figures. He has also highlighted his involvement in a non-profit organization, which always adds value to his qualifications.

Joan White
6 Hope Street
Anytown, CA 55555
555-123-4567

January 8, 20XX

Ms. Sue Jones
Marketing Manager
ABC Company
1234 First Street
Anytown, CA 55555

LETTER 2: Reentry Into Job Market
Response to an Ad
Traditional Style using Bullets

Dear Ms. Jones:

I am responding to your ad published in the ABC Times, dated January 5, 20XX, for the position of Administrative Manager, Reference #123456.

This is exactly the sort of job I want and for which I believe I am qualified. As listed in your ad, my skills match those you seek.

Computer Literacy
I am computer proficient and have mastered spreadsheet programs (familiar with budgets, IF-functions, macro functions), and with word processing programs (familiar with layout, merge, mass mailing functions).

Planning Skills
Managing a 6-dentist practice for 8 years I maintained all patient schedules, handled payroll, material ordering and distribution, printing and reproduction, and records management.

Leadership
In the last 5 years, I have been coordinator of a 32-team softball league and have been the chairperson for two large charity fundraisers to benefit organizations in my community, raising over $125,000 on average each year.

Educational Background
I have an Associate Degree in Science, with a major in Business Administration.

I will call you the morning of January 15th to find a time that might be mutually beneficial for a meeting to further explore your needs, or you may reach me at 555-123-4567, would you prefer to contact me upon receipt of my letter.

Sincerely,

Joan White

Joan White

COMMENTS: The author of this letter has put the emphasis on the positive contributions she can offer, rather than focusing on the years she has been out of the work force. She lists her skills and qualifications in "skill language" rather than in "job titles". She stays with the job requirements and shows more current and relevant experience under leadership skills, which proves she has stayed active and can manage others, drawing from her volunteer activities. These skills are transferable to this job.

By not enclosing her resume, which would immediately focus an employer on the gap in paid employment (if using a chronological format), she is more likely to be invited for a meeting. In a meeting, she will have a chance to highlight how she is qualified for this job, despite this gap.

John Smith
6 Hope Street
Anytown, CA 55555
555-123-4567

January 1, 20XX

Mr. Joe Jones
Owner
ABC Landscaping Company
1234 First Street
Anytown, CA 55555

Dear Mr. Jones:

Mr. Paul Brown, a customer of yours for 8 years, mentioned that you had a growth rate of 12% and might be looking for someone with diversified experience. Paul and I have been members in the "Fast Wheel Bicycle Club" for many years and often ride together. When he mentioned your company, I was very impressed by his praise for the originality of your work.

I have decided to offer my services to a company like yours that operates in the field of landscaping for private properties. In the last decade, I have acquired experience in three fields that, I think, are of interest to you - Administrative, Production, and Sales.

Administrative: I worked on computer-designed landscapes, as well as mastering spreadsheets for planning and accounting purposes. I checked suppliers' invoices (up to 60 a week) for accuracy, and adapted a software program to invoice customers (up to 3000 lines per month).

Production: I coordinated the work of seven cleaning crews with an average of 15 unskilled workers on each crew, kept inventory by taking stock each month, prepared order sheets, and reduced theft from 3.2% to 1.2% in consumer goods.

Sales: I conducted phones sales of insurance and was ranked three times as Salesman of the Month. I have experience as a real estate agent with a 15% average success rate for listing contracts vs. the company average of 11%.

I am most interested in the opportunity to meet with you and discuss how I might make a positive contribution to your company. I will call you next week to see when you have time for a meeting.

Sincerely,

John Smith

John Smith

COMMENTS: The writer of this letter has lumped together the bulk of his experience under three headings which highlight both the diversity of his experience (a plus for any company) and the complimentary and overlapping nature of those skills. This is always important in a smaller company where being a "jack of all trades" is often necessary. In this way, he does not have to dwell on the number of jobs he's had in the past (in his case, 7), but rather focuses on the areas of experience and expertise he acquired in those jobs, as seen in their totality.

In addition, he uses his relationship with one of this employer's customers as the starting point to approach the employer.

Paul Jones
6 Hope Street
Anytown, CA 55555
555-123-4567

January 1, 20XX

Mr. Sam Smith
V.P. of Marketing
ABC Company
1234 First Street
Anytown, CA 55555

Dear Mr. Smith:

After looking at your web site, I have discovered three possible projects I could carry out for your company in an 8 to 12 week internship period or on a project basis.

Potential Project 1 - Pricing Strategy

Research and formulate a pricing strategy to gain a larger market share for those of your products in the highly competitive markets flooded by South Asian products of average quality.

Potential Project 2 - New Packaging Options

Conduct a systematic survey of the packaging options that are currently being used for consumer goods like these in First World Countries, such as the United States, Canada, Sweden, and Italy. Make a realistic proposal on how to implement these packaging concepts to enhance your existing products.

Potential Project 3 - Product Comparisons

Compare the products of your leading competitors to determine the 3 key advantages and 3 key disadvantages of each and make recommendations for each of your similar products. This will allow for better positioning in the market. In addition, I will interview both resellers and end users for recommendations to increase sales.

I will be in your area next month and will call you in one week to set up a meeting to further discuss these proposals.

Sincerely,

Paul Jones

Paul Jones

COMMENTS: Many companies don't take advantage of internships or short project contracts because they are uncertain what kind of projects could reasonably be carried out in such a short time frame. The author offers three diverse alternatives that outline the potential benefits of each to the employer. By offering 3 projects, he multiplies his chances by 3 (as it is likely that one of three will interest the employer). The author of this letter has suggested projects the employer might not otherwise be able to accomplish due to timing or staff limitations, but would be ideal for a short-term contract person.

Joan White
6 Hope Street
Anytown, CA 55555
555-123-4567

January 8, 20XX

Ms. Sue Jones
Owner
ABC Company
1234 First Street
Anytown, CA 55555

Dear Ms. Jones:

If you like paradox, I can offer you an example. Like any company in the field of tourism, you may suffer from high turnover of employees who work for you in the field of graphic communication.

I was born in Lebanon, educated in France, and currently live in San Francisco. My background has allowed me to speak Arabic, French and English fluently, and I have a good command of Spanish and Italian. I have always been fascinated by the diversity of cultures.

A proficiency in MS Publisher, Quark Express, In-Design, Macromedia Studio 8, J2SE and Word, allows me to produce any communication materials you might need. I have worked in a small design company of 35 employees, based on the West Coast, with design responsibilities for websites, animation, identity and collateral materials.

As a travel consultant for Higher Learning Tours, I worked for many years as a lecturer and guide, participating in over 35 different tours.

I have decided to offer my services on a long-term basis to a medium sized company specializing in cultural tours for upper middle class travelers. I am a military spouse and have moved, as an average every 2.9 years, but I have discovered how to overcome this fact and offer stability (hence the paradox!) The variety of services I can offer you do not require me to be on your premises, but I can be relied on to do any job needed in a timely fashion. I offer not only my skills as a designer, but my ability to lead tours on a 30-45% time basis.

Being very flexible, I am at your disposal to visit you in Anytown at your convenience. I would welcome a meeting to further discuss my interest in your company.

Sincerely,

Joan White

Joan White

COMMENTS: The author of this letter turns what might be perceived by some as the negative feature of constantly moving due to a military lifestyle, into a positive solution by suggesting a permanent working relationship that doesn't require her physical presence in an office. Her highly mobile life might suggest that she would leave after a short tenure, but her solution overcomes this difficulty.

Sue Parker
6 Hope Street
Anytown, CA 55555
555-123-4567

January 1, 20XX

Mr. Joe Jones
Manager of Housing Developments
Jones Construction
1234 First Street
Anytown, CA 55555

> **LETTER 6:** Lack of Formal Education
> Lower Level Accounting Assistant Job
> Ad Placed by Employer but Responding
> as Though Ad Wasn't Seen (Sometimes
> Called a "False" Unsolicited Letter)
> Use of Bullets

Dear Mr. Jones:

I read in an article posted on the ABC Times site that your company won the bid to build the new housing development in Anytown, which is due to open in June of 2008. This may neccesitate an increase in your accounting team of dedicated and enthusiastic employees.

I have always worked in small to medium sized companies, like yours, in the construction business. In my last job I was responsible for:

- Matching all supplier invoices with orders - $5 million purchases per year;
- Scheduling work crews of 3 to 12 people for weekly assignments;
- Preparing weekly reports dealing with profitability statements and cash management with +/- 5% deviation as an average;
- Negotiating and optimizing financial rates with 5 banks for up to a 15% discount of the original rate;
- Analyzing the top 20% key customer accounts that made up 80% of revenue and making recommendations for additional services.

I have acquired all my skills in the years I have worked since graduating from high school. In each job I have held, I have proven I am results-oriented, respectful of target dates and able to set priorities – sometimes by extinguishing fires! I am sure you will appreciate the wisdom and efficiency gained in my career compensate for the lack of a specific degree.

I will take the initiative to call you next week.

Sincerely,

Sue Parker

Sue Parker

COMMENTS: The author of this letter has found an ad for a job she would like, but for which she misses one key qualification – an educational degree. Instead of using a traditional approach and sending her application to H.R. as other candidates will do who are responding to the ad, she bypasses them and sends a "false" unsolicited letter to the line manager, whose name she has found by phoning the company prior to writing. She writes without reference to the ad, so her letter will not be automatically routed to H.R. who may likely screen her out because she lacks a degree. The line manager, however, may appreciate that what she offers matches the job requirements in more valuable and relevant ways and can appraise her unique experience for the job.

Sue Jones
6 Hope Street
Anytown, CA 55555
555-123-1456

November 3, 20XX

Mr. Sam Smith
Office Manager
ABC Company
1234 First Street
Anytown, CA 55555

Re: Your ad in the ABC Times, dated November 1, 20XX, for the position of Receptionist, Job Reference #45678B

Dear Mr. Smith,

I read your ad for the receptionist position at your company. This letter expresses my interest in the position you have to fill.

Prior to writing this letter to you, I did two things:

- I visited your office and was impressed by its wheelchair accessibility.
- I discovered your company's interest in and support of the Special Olympics.

On the basis of those two observations, I gather you are a group of people who understand the uniqueness and capabilities of those of us in wheelchairs.

You ad requires someone with the five following qualifications:

You Need:	I have:
Social Skills	During my work as a claims processor, I developed **three techniques** to deal with customers in stressful situations, which are still in use at the company.
Capacity to answer phones, diagnosis needs and route call to proper person	In Computer XZY Company, I handled **heavy volume calls** – 20 to 50 per hour, listened to customer comments and directed call to the appropriate extension.
Language Skills	I speak **English and Spanish** fluently
Reliability	In my fourteen years of experience (3500 days), I have been absent only 5 days.
Memorize faces and names.	I can easily recognize over 300 faces and remember names; on the telephone I can identify more than 50 people by their voice alone.

I am available to meet with you at your convenience. I would welcome a call at 555-123-4567 to set up a meeting.

Thank you very much for your interest.

Sincerely,

Sue Jones

Sue Jones

COMMENTS: The author of this letter knows she must mention the fact of her physical limitation right away. She does this elegantly and moves on immediately by listing how she is qualified for the job. She has shown that she knows the company's location is wheelchair accessible, so the employer will not have to make any accommodations, were he to hire her. She also shows her enthusiasm by visiting the company prior to writing and finding out about their involvement with the Special Olympics. She demonstrates that she is a person who goes the extra mile.

The use of the Mirror Style is effective in quickly showing her suitability for the job by matching, point-for-point, the skills needed (those listed in the ad) with her qualifications. She uses the reference line to list the details about the ad, so the recipient knows immediately the job for which she is applying.

Mr. Stan Smith
6 Hope Street
Anytown, CA 55555
555-123-4567

October 15, 20XX

Mr. Joe Jones
Marketing Manager
ABC Film Festival
1234 First Street
Anytown, CA 55555

Dear Mr. Jones:

The ABC Film Festival has firmly established itself as the premiere event of its kind in Anytown. I read that over 3,500 people attended the screenings at this year's event.

Reaching out on a limited budget of $27,000 is extremely challenging for the film festival that you coordinate. In my previous role in charge of marketing at XYZ Company, we experienced a similar issue.

I am currently an MBA student at Big Valley University, with a specialization in Entertainment Strategy. I have undertaken a study of effective marketing tools as part of an internship project with the Regional Film Institute. This study resulted in 25 concrete recommendations, which I believe would be of interest to you. I have enclosed the outline of this project.

I can be reached at the number below and will certainly appreciate the chance to meet with you and discuss this further.

Yours sincerely,

Stan Smith

Stan Smith
555-123-4567

Enclosure: Marketing Project Outline for the Regional Film Institute

COMMENTS: The author of this letter establishes his interest and knowledge of this event. He mentions his marketing background and his MBA studies, but focuses the letter on his desire to share recommendations from a study he conducted during his internship. He encloses the outline from the study to demonstrate his seriousness and hopefully pique the recipient's interest to learn more.

Sue Smith
6 Hope Street
Anytown, CA 44444
555-123-4567

January 1, 20XX

Chair and Selection Committee
Anytown Community College
Anytown, USA 22222

RE: Your ad published in the ABC Times on Nov. 2nd 20XX, for the position of Student
    Services Coordinator, Job Number 12345

To the Chair and Selection Committee,

I am very excited about the Student Services Coordinator position at Anytown Community
College! My business friend and past associate, John Smith, Dean of Instruction at Big Valley
Community College, thought I would be ideal for this position and suggested I contact
you immediately. Listed below are your stated qualifications and how my skills, education
and experience meet each of these qualifications. My love of education and my belief in its
importance to the community cannot be over emphasized. Education provides the springboard needed to meet the many challenges presented to every person in this life.

JOB REQUIRES:	I HAVE:
Knowledge of Higher Education Policies and Practices	Recruited (500+ per year) and advised (200+ per year) students at the University of Anytown – UOA - 4 years
Establishing Relationships with Diverse Populations	Set up foundation for and maintained working relationships with 15 high schools, 3 community colleges and 7 local businesses while working at the ABC Company – 4 years, and UOA – 4 years
Develop Presentations, Organize and Maintain Records	Developed and presented a variety of training and marketing materials (15 different programs), organized and maintained records for 2000 students
Effective Oral and Communication Skills	Over 15 years of speaking experience with organizations, students, educators - large and small groups; taught for Lone Ridge College-Business Communications Course – Current Year
College Degree/Master Preferred	Master in Public Administration, with counseling emphasis, Anytown University Bachelor of Arts in Psychology

I am very interested in joining the recruiter/enrollment team. I will call you during the
week of November 17th to the 21st to arrange a convenient time for a meeting. Thank
you for your time and consideration.

Sincerely,

Sue Smith

Sue Smith

COMMENTS: The author of this letter is responding to an ad for a job in a community
college. She lists the job name and number in the reference line. She knows the letter will
go to a committee, so her salutation is to the group instead of a specific person. She has
used the mirror style to list how her qualifications meet the exact job description, using
quantifiable results. She does not enclose a resume, as she is returning to the work force
after raising her children. Instead of listing the years of her experience at each job, she
lists the number of years she worked at each job. This shows she has over 15 years of
experience, which should be much more impressive to the committee than the fact she
has a gap in employment.

Bill Smith
1234 Second Street
Anytown, USA 44444

November 1, 20XX

Joe Redford
V.P. of Customer Service
ABC Fine Homes
3456 Cedar Street
Anytown, USA 55555

Dear Mr. Redford:

The magazine "Management Today" highlights your 212% rate of growth in their article "How to be Successful in a Buyer's Market?" (October 20XX). This is the reason I am writing you. I have been following your activities over the last two years with interest and admiration.

In companies facing the same sort of challenges and competition as yours, I have been instrumental over the last 9 years in developing and implementing answers to "hot issues." Among others, these are three projects that I carried out:

I conducted a needs analysis survey among the employees to identify the three key reasons to explain the high turnover that affected this company. On the basis of this survey, management made operational and strategic decisions. Within a twelve-month period, the turnover rate went down from 11% to 7%.

I developed a three-day (2 + 1) negotiation seminar to increase the success rate of sales calls. The average monthly sales, per person, went up from $62,000 to $95,000, after six months from the program's implementation date.

Using John Holland's typology as the defining principle, the sales force, under my leadership, developed a diversified sales promotion brochure to address each one of the six types of customers. Three years later the entire sales force is still using this approach to better understand how to address the needs of each type of customer and missed sales have dropped from 32% to 18%.

I will be visiting Anytown in the second half of this month and I will take the initiative to call you next week to arrange a meeting.

Sincerely,

Bill Smith

Bill Smith

COMMENTS: The author of this letter mentions an article he has read about the company he is approaching. He lists three key points about his background that might interest the recipient and uses concrete results to illustrate his qualifications. He does not live in the same city as this company but will be visiting it in the near future, so mentions this in the follow-up paragraph. He is planning ahead to line up a meeting for his visit.

Bill White
6 Hope Street
Anytown, CA 55555
555-123-4567

January 26, 20XX

Mr. Steve Smith
Accounting Supervisor
ABC Company
1234 First Street
Anytown, CA 55555

Dear Mr. Smith:

During the international exhibition on "Body Care" in Toronto earlier this month, I had the pleasure to meet with you at your booth. You suggested I contact you after the 25th of this month, when you would be back at your office. This is the reason for my letter.

You asked me to send some information about my background.

- For the last 7 years, I have worked as an auditor and prior to that, I worked for 4 years as an administrative assistant.

- I have an accounting background and possess a diploma from the International School for Auditors in Anytown.

- I carry both American and Canadian passports.

- I speak several languages: French (my mother tongue), German and English fluently.

- I am very flexible in terms of geography, and would be willing to move for the right opportunity.

I would be very happy to meet with you and talk further about my background and interest in your company. Thank you, again, for your openness and willingness to talk with me at the exhibition.

I can be reached at 555-123-4567.

Sincerely,

Bill White

Bill White

COMMENTS: The author of this letter has followed up, at the request of the recipient, after meeting at a trade show. This letter should be short and emphasize the points of interest covered in their discussion at that first meeting. Limit it to 5 points, no more. The recipient is already interested or would not have asked for a follow-up, so only cover what is of most interest and do not try to over sell. The important thing in this instance to make sure you follow up as you promised. Do not miss an opportunity when you have already established contact. The hard part is over!

Ms. Sue Jones
6 Hope Street
Anytown, CA 55555
555-123-4567

July 1, 20XX

Mr. Sam Smith
Operations Manager
ABC Company
1234 First Street
Anytown, CA 55555

Dear Mr. Smith:

Ms. Janet Brown suggested I write you to express my interest in the position of a service clerk, which I understand is currently available.

I am delighted to apply for this position, which is very similar in nature to the last three jobs I have had at the companies listed below. Also listed are some of my key responsibilities in each of those jobs.

Organization	Characteristics	Responsibilites
ABC Garage 555-123-4567	27 Employees Sales of New and Used Vehicles	1. Responsible for organizing bi-weekly meetings 2. Planning weekly schedules 3. Delivering Information to the clientele (40+ per day)
BCD Supermarket 555-234-5678	Grocery Chain with $2 Million in Yearly Sales	1. Placing 50 orders per day 2. Handling customer comments and complaints (flow of 300+ per day) 3. Following up on 10+ deliveries daily
CDE Hospital 555-345-6789	Emergency Room Front Desk in 150 Bed Hospital	1. Receiving 50 to 250 telephone calls a day 2. Routing calls to proper depart-ment (80% in less than 20 seconds) 3. Paging needed personnel 4. Filing Paperwork (100+ docu-ments per day)

I will take the initiative to call your assistant at the beginning of next week to arrange for a meeting with you.

Sincerely,

Sue Jones

Sue Jones

> **LETTER 12:** Service Clerk Job
> By Referral
> Matrix Design

COMMENTS: The author of this letter chose to use a matrix design, which will quickly provide the reader with pertinent and quantified facts. It's convincing and striking in its simplicity and readability. For jobs where tasks and responsibilities are easily categorized, it is a good style to adopt. The author has also listed phone numbers for her past employers as a sign of her confidence that they will speak well of her if the recipient calls them.

Bill White
6 Hope Street
Anytown, CA 55555
555-123-4567

June 1, 20XX

Mr. Steve Smith
Credit Department Manager
International Bank Company
1234 First Street
Anytown, CA 55555

Dear Mr. Smith:

In an article in The Times yesterday, I read that you are:

1.   Expanding your international strategy team in the credit card sector.

2.   Finding it hard to find qualified personnel in Los Angeles with previous international experience in this area.

I have been working in the Los Angeles banking sector for over six years, first with ABC Bank, and more recently with XYZ Bank, with a particular focus on **developing their international credit card activities** by marketing to their small business consumer client base. While with XYZ Bank, I increased the **penetration of their credit card sales from 8% to 25%** among their customer base. Our campaigns also had a 5% contribution to the sales growth within flagship branches.

I have a Masters Degree in International Finance, and prior to moving to Los Angeles lived in **London** for three years where I worked at Bank One. I attended school in **Paris** for my undergraduate degree, and speak French fluently.

I would appreciate the opportunity to further discuss this matter with you and will give you a call in the next couple of days to set up a meeting.

Sincerely,

Bill White

Bill White

COMMENTS: The author of this letter zeros in on the employer's priorities and makes sure he quantifies the results he has achieved for others and that those results are congruent and in the magnitude of the employer's universe. He shows his international connections and takes the initiative to follow up. He uses **Bold** to emphasize key words.

Stan Smith
6 Hope Street
Anytown, CA 55555
555-123-4567

> **LETTER 14:** Unsolicited Letter
> You-Me-We Approach

May 15, 20XX

Mr. Joe Jones
Route Scheduler
Jones Delivery and Moving
1234 First Street
Anytown, CA 55555

Dear Mr. Jones:

In a particularly difficult economic time, your company has been able to **grow by 7%** while most of your industry has suffered from an average **decline of 4%**. This is the reason I have decided to send you my application for inventory control and delivery person.

At the ABC Company, I was responsible for furniture **inventory control of over 2500 items**, on average.

As a driver/delivery person with the XYZ Company, I managed to organize **5 deliveries** a day, versus the 3.5 they were making when I joined them, and **completed 89%** within the time set for each one.

In the service of GHI Company, I was in charge of quality control and the conditioning and packaging of widgets for use in the repair of home fixtures. I maintained **a productivity rate above 92%**.

I will call you this week, on Tuesday, to arrange a meeting to further discuss these points.

Sincerely,

Stan Smith

Stan Smith

COMMENTS: The author of this unsolicited letter has mentioned something positive about the company and shown his interest in them. The nature of this job seeks precision and efficiency, so the author has used examples that highlight these exact features, by using concrete facts and figures to demonstrate results.

Joan White
6 Hope Street
Anytown, CA 55555
555-123-4567

January 8, 20XX

Ms. Sue Jones
Owner
ABC Store
1234 First Street
Anytown, CA 55555

Dear Ms. Jones:

By visiting your store at least twice a month over the last several years, I have noticed the importance you and your staff place on welcoming your customers and the thoughtful service that you provide.

Working for 3 years for Foods, Inc., a large food market, I was responsible for the produce section of fruits and vegetables. During that time, I was able to **increase sales by 10%** by my second year due to rigorous control of the quality of these products and **improving the selection** of goods offered.

I served more than 30 customers a day in addition to my regular duties, by taking and fulfilling **special orders** for birthdays, holidays, parties and special functions. The sales in this particular sector **jumped from $750,000 to $1,300,000** in my 3 years, largely due to a special birthday promotional campaign I launched to bring in orders.

Understanding that the role of any store is to welcome and to serve their customers in a friendly atmosphere, I would like to bring all my competence and enthusiasm in the service of your company and to meet the needs of your clientele.

I would welcome the chance to talk further with you about my interest. I will call you on February 18th to set a date and a time.

Sincerely,

Joan White

Joan White

COMMENTS: The author of this letter has highlighted examples from her past to show she understands the economic as well as social side of this kind of job. She stresses the importance of welcoming customers and providing quality service and uses facts and figures to show how she has taken the initiative in her past jobs to do that. She does not mention a particular job title because there are two job possibilities she is interested in and would need to talk with the recipient before deciding which is the better fit.

Sue Jones
6 Hope Street
Anytown, CA 55555
555-123-4567

July 3, 20XX

Mr. Joe Black
Editorial Manager
ABC Publishing
1234 First Street
Anytown, CA 55555

> **LETTER 16:** Response to an Ad for a
> Job Not Previously Held
> Use of Bullets

RE: Your ad in the Sunday Times, dated July 1, 20XX, for a Proofreader, Job Number 5678Z

Dear Mr. Black,

The choice of a manuscript, the editing process, reporduction, and distribution are the key tasks for the job of proofreader that you seek to fill. These tasks interest and excite me and that is why I am writing to you.

I think I am uniquely suited to this job based on the following qualifications.

1. **Reviewer** – my love of books and the written word prompted me to write reviews of the current fiction bestsellers for the Daily Press in Anytown. More recently, I have expanded these reviews to run in Everytown's Variety newspaper. I am fascinated by literature and interested in the process of how a book is published and in the care brought to its development.

2. **Teaching Credential** – I taught American and English Literature at ABC High School in River City. This experience allowed me to share my passion with students who eventually managed to read an average of one book every two weeks, up from under one book per month.

3. **Ph.D. in English Literature and Art History** – I wrote an interdisciplinary report on English poet and engraver, William Blake, of the 16th century. I followed this up by editing the works of two of my colleagues: one paper on English literature, and one paper on art history. My attention to detail and my exacting concern for the proper use of words helped me to excel at these tasks.

As you requested, I have enclosed my resume.

I would be happy to develop these and other points with you during a meeting. I will call you next week to arrange a convenient date and time.

Sincerely,

Sue Jones

Sue Jones

Enc: Resume

COMMENTS: The author of this letter is responding to an ad for a job she has not held before. This is perfectly fine if it can be demonstrated that her skills and interests closely relate to the work she would do if hired. She must show that her skills are transferable to the job she seeks. She uses a bullet-style letter to highlight the three qualifications she possesses which make her a good candidate for this job. Of course, as a proofreader, there cannot be even one error in her letter! She encloses her resume since the ad requested it, after having tailored it by deleting details that are not relevant to this particular job.

John Smith
6 Hope Street
Anytown, CA 55555
555-123-4567

January 1, 20XX

Ms. Sue Jones
Cuisine Restaurant
1234 First Street
Anytown, CA 55555

Dear Ms. Jones:

> **LETTER 17:** Unsolicited Letter
> With Enclosures to Support Statements
> Use of Bullets

I am a fan of your restaurant, *Cuisine* . Your "Pamplemousse Tart" is famous through-out Anytown, and is a particular favorite of mine. I know that your customers receive impeccable service and outstanding quality when they dine with you. This is why I have written to offer my services as a chef.

- I was chef at Rivera restaurant from 19XX to 20XX. I was responsible for all aspects of food preparation, menu planning, provisioning, quality and execution. My particular specialty was in the design and creation of new dishes and in the crafting of specialized menus for banquets and special events. I have enclosed a sample menu from my restaurant.

- I am aware of the stringent standards for a safe and sanitary work environment that conform to standardized and approved regulations, and have always applied all necessary safe handing procedures. Kitchens under my supervision have never received warnings from the Health Department.

- For special events, I organized and prepared meals for well over 1000 guests. I have enclosed pictures of 7 of my buffet designs.

- I have a degree from the ABC Culinary Institute. I was guest chef on the local program "Today in Anytown" in September 20XX. I am a member of the American Culinary Federation. I have enclosed two articles that appeared in our local papers about my activities.

My professional objectives are to collaborate with others to maintain high quality food and service, to participate in the increase of profitability and create a good working atmosphere.

I will take the initiative to call you for a meeting.

Sincerely,

John Smith

John Smith

Enc: Sample Menu
Enc: 7 pictures of buffet receptions
Enc: 2 Press Articles

COMMENTS: The author of this letter has enclosed important material to illustrate his claims. Do not hesitate to enclose material that will show the recipient proof of what you say. Send copies of special documents or pictures that highlight a particular aspect of your work. As is the case here, where food is a highly visual commodity, these pictures can, in just seconds, show the author's expertise. Make sure the quality of your enclosures is good – do not send fuzzy or poorly reproduced materials. Send enough to make your case, but reserve some material for a meeting.

Sue Smith
6 Hope Street
Anytown, CA 55555
555-123-4567

March 20, 20XX

Mr. Joe Small
New Accounts
Food-to-You
1234 First Street
Anytown, CA 55555

Dear Mr. Jones:

I am currently a student at Anytown University, majoring in Business and will graduate in three months. I am very interested in your company and know that your online food business grew by 34% last year. I read an article about your plans for expansion into the dairy market (The Times, October 10, 20XX) and this is why I am writing to you.

While in college, I set up an online company to deliver fresh produce to customers who had difficulty getting to the grocery store. In June of last year, I sold my company to a larger competitor to concentrate on my studies and make plans for my next career move. Below are three examples of my accomplishments.

Problem:	People without transportation cannot get fresh produce
Action:	Founded EasyProduce, an online retail fresh food business
Result:	Within first year, **gained 500 new customers** within Anytown

Problem:	Needed productive operational system to deliver food
Action:	Arranged with delivery service to use their vans
Result:	Partnering with existing company allowed for **92% on-time deliveries**

Problem:	How to manage diverse teams of people
Action:	Set up work incentive program to earn bonuses
Result:	**Turnover was only 4%** in first year of operation

My professional objective is to work for a company whose major goal is customer satisfaction. I would be pleased to meet with you and further discuss the points above. I will take the initiative to call you on April 1st to arrange for a time we might meet.

Sincerely,

Sue Smith

Sue Smith

> **LETTER 18:** Unsolicited Letter –
> Using Problem/Action/Result Format
> College Student

COMMENTS: The author of this letter is a college student about to graduate, who started a business. She is writing an unsolicited letter using a style that highlights her skills. She mentions a problem, the action taken to meet the problem, and the result of the action, using quantifiable facts. This style is very clear and focuses the reader immediately on her qualifications.

Sue Jones
6 Hope Street
Anytown, CA 55555
555-123-4567

January 8, 20XX

Ms. Pam Smith
Manager
XYZ Clothes Store
1234 First Street
Anytown, CA 55555

Dear Ms. Smith:

I have appreciated the pleasant atmosphere of your store, as well as the professionalism of your sales staff. I have purchased two of my favorite blouses at your store during my visits as a customer. This has motivated me to write to you and offer my services as a sales clerk.

I have always had a love for fashion and an ability to sell products. I have 14 months of experience as a specialized saleswoman and sales assistant at ABC Clothes Shoppe at River Valley Mall. I managed the shop with one other colleague, and was responsible for opening on time, sales displays, serving customers and for reconciling the **daily receipts of $5,500** +/- for deposit each night.

Our team of 7 persons served approximately **200 customers a day, with a 60% sales rate** once we had established rapport. We also handled approximately 2 complaints a day concerning the after-sales service, when goods were either defective or didn't match customer expectations.

I am comfortable selling most products, once I have been thoroughly trained on their advantages and features. I consider the role of the salesperson to be knowledge-able and enthusiastic while serving others.

I would like to put my enthusiasm and passion to work for you and will call you on May 15th to see when I might be able to come by and talk with you about my offer.

Thank you very much.

Sincerely,

Sue Jones

Sue Jones

COMMENTS: The author of this letter has very little experience but fleshes out what she does have in several ways. She is acquainted with the employer and mentions this to open the door. She must convey her enthusiasm and passion for this work since she has only had one job.

Stan Smith
6 Hope Street
Anytown, CA 55555
555-123-4567

February 17, 20XX

Mr. Joe Jones
Hotel Operations Manager
1234 First Street
Anytown, CA 55555

Dear Mr. Jones:

> **Assistant General Manager**
> Reference: Job #33rr5
>
> 3 Years Experience required in Hotel Management and Marketing; must speak French and English fluently; ability to work alone necessary; must have customer service as first priority; degree in Hospitality Management a plus, but not necessary.
> Send resume to:
> Joe Jones at 1234 First Street, Anytown, CA 55555
> Salary commensurate with experience.

In response to the above published ad, I possess the 5 characteristics you have listed.

1. **Mastery of English and French**
   English is my mother tongue. I lived in France for 12 years, during which I time I attended school and learned to speak and write French fluently.

2. **University Degree in Hospitality Management**
   I have a degree in Hospitality Management from the University of Anytown, 20XX.

3. **Three Years of Experience**
   I worked for the White Sands Hotel for two years. I was responsible for the Mediterranean market and was charged with increasing our customer base to bring in more conferences. During this period, sales increased by more than 30% a year. I worked for two years for ABC Company and specialized in the distribution of secondary services for hotels and restaurants, resulting in a 52% increase per year in sales.

4. **Autonomous and Independent**
   At my last job, I was given the responsibility to set my own objectives and manage my budget with autonomy and independence. While my job required extensive personal contact with the customer base, my interaction with my hierarchy was limited to one working day per month for goal setting and planning. Most of my communication was essentially made by email or phone.

5. **Customer Minded**
   My professional success is largely due to " the customer culture " that I continuously maintained and developed. In my last job, I implemented a Customers' Club to allow the exchange of business networking and the implementation of systems for "Benchmarking". This resulted in an increase in the development of customer loyalty from 41% to 72% in 2 years, as measured by return visits.

I would be delighted to develop one or more of the points during a meeting with you. I can be reached at 555-123-4567.

Sincerely,

Stan Smith

Stan Smith

Enc.: Resume

LETTER 20: Imbedding an Ad – Point by Point Use of Bullets

COMMENTS: The author of this letter has used a "sensitivity approach" by imbedding a copy of the actual ad into the page. The ad was scanned, reduced and placed in the letter at the top. Since a copy of the ad is in the letter, the author does not need to use the reference line to identify the job. Each of the criteria from the ad is addressed, point for point. He presents them under titles to strengthen the "Question-answer" effect. He includes a short tailored resume since it has been requested, but the selling and convincing has been done in the body of the letter.

John Smith
6 Hope Street
Anytown, CA 55555
555-123-4567

November 2, 20XX

Ms. Sue Jones
Marketing Manager
ABC Company
1234 First Street
Anytown, CA 55555

Dear Ms. Jones:

I want to thank you for the interest you demonstrated in me during our meeting on November 1st, 20XX.

I would like to reiterate my interest in the position of Customer Relations Manager. I am convinced that I have both the skills and enthusiasm to do this job. After our conversation, I understand your three priorities for this job are:

- Clean and enrich the data warehouse for your type B customers (students);
- Prepare and conduct 1 or 2 mass mailings per week to acquire new customers in college and university settings;
- Improve customer loyalty for your high-end products by at least 20%.

You mentioned you will be making your decision on the 25th of this month. I can be reached at 555-123-4567 and look forward to your call.

Again, thank you for your time and interest.

Sincerely,

John Smith

John Smith

COMMENTS: A thank you letter after every meeting is a MUST. It is better, in almost all cases, that you do not send a handwritten note, as it is too informal. Ideally, you should send a hard copy of your letter so it can be kept in your file.

The thank you letter shows your good manners and demonstrates your continued interest in the job. This is the place to show that you have understood what the job entails, and that you are aware of their top priorities and have sensitivity to them. In one sentence reiterate your desire for the job, but do not list your qualifications again. If you have done your job well in the interview or meeting, they will know how you are qualified. The letter is to show your appreciation for their time and interest and that you listened to them during the meeting.

When all other things are equal and an employer cannot decide which candidate to hire, sending a thank you note can tip the advantage to your side.

Appendix C
Unsolicited Letter Quiz
Answers and Rationale

Listed below are the answers to the quiz at the beginning of Chapter 5. Some issues are more gray than black and white, so it isn't possible to say that in every instance one choice will always be better than the other. These answers are meant to be guidelines, and we offer from two to seven reasons for every answer selected that support why we have chosen it as the better of the two choices.

1. **If you have the choice, use:**

   ☑ **The recipient's name rather than their title** because:
   - A name is more personal than a title.
   - Titles can change (as a result of promotions), whereas names rarely ever change.
   - It is more pleasant and less formal.
   - Your letter is more likely to reach the right person.
   - This prevents your letter from being screened out by a secretary/assistant.

2. **You make sure to give:**

   ☑ **Examples of your achievements, results, and evidence** because:
   - Interviewers are more interested in your achievements, than in the titles you have held.
   - In business, what you say is more interesting than the way you say it (results over style).
   - Two identical titles might conceal two very different achievements.
   - People can achieve amazing things without ever being awarded titles.
   - This sets the discussion topics for a meeting.
   - This gives an idea of your capabilities.
   - This shows that you have experience.

3. **You send your letter to:**

   ☑ **Whoever is most appropriate** because:
   - Those in your field of expertise are more easily convinced by your professionalism; they can understand and evaluate your skills and achievements.
   - Personnel departments deal with a lot of applications, and competition is fierce.
   - It is easier to convince someone who is in the same field as yourself than it is to convince someone who does not understand your field.
   - Your skills will interest them personally.

4. **You start your letter:**

☑ **By mentioning a subject/issue which affects the organization and/or the recipient** because:

- Otherwise, your reader is not really interested.
- This attracts their immediate attention.
- This lets you open and direct discussions during a meeting.
- This encourages them to continue reading your letter.

5. **You think that it is worthwhile:**

☑ **Not to include a stamped self-sddressed envelope for their answer** because:

- This is no longer a common practice.
- Organizations can easily afford the price of a stamp.
- Your envelope might not necessarily suit the size of their paper.
- Your objective is a meeting; a telephone call to/from them is better than receiving a return letter.
- This may look as if you don't trust them to take the iniatitive to get back in touch with you, so you are sending the means for it (they may use the phone to follow up when they are interested and feel the envelope is a waste).

6. **In your letter, you specify that you are looking for:**

☑ **a 20-minute meeting** because:

- To be successful, you should break down your final objective (getting a job) into intermediate objectives (getting a first meeting).
- You will never be hired by way of the letter alone; hiring decisions are made after one job meeting, at the very least.
- You actually want to meet your recipient to determine if you like them and really want the job.
- You want your face to become familiar to your recipient.

7. **As well as your cover letter:**

☑ **You should not include your resume** because:

- When responding to an ad, they may ask for your resume; when approaching a company spontaneously, they do not ask for anything.
- Your resume may include irrelevant and potentially damaging information which could lead to you being screened out.
- It is better to bring it with you to a meeting.

- you want to pique their curiosity.
- it may never be asked for (or needed).
- a meeting is more important than a resume.

8. In your letter:

☑ **You describe yourself in two or three lines, using information which may interest your recipient** because:

- You should always assume that your reader has very little time to give you; therefore, it is very important to be relevant.
- By concentrating on what is essential, you demonstrate your professionalism (and prevent yourself from getting bogged down in details).
- The briefness and conciseness of your letter will be appreciated by your reader.
- This prevents you from boring them.
- This shows that you know how to highlight the most important things about yourself.
- You can anticipate and meet their expectations.

9. If the person that you want to meet is very important:

☑ **You approach them, for the first time, via their secretary/assistant** because:

- This eliminates the risk of an on-the-spot telephone meeting.
- If you don't get them to help you, you can still try to reach the person directly.
- If you ask very technical questions (when appropriate), they may not be able to answer them and will have to pass you on to the person directly.
- This prevents you from being judged quickly.
- You can get more information.
- It is good practice before a meeting.
- They may quicken the process and introduce you in a better light to your interviewer.

10. Your letters should be:

☑ **Typed** because:

- This prevents them from studying your handwriting without you knowing it.
- This lets your interviewer spend more time reading about your achievements than trying to understand what you have written.
- This makes your document look very professional.

- This shows that you are a "Resource Person" and not a "Job-Beggar."
- this is quicker and looks better.
- this is easier to read.

11. If you don't get an answer:

☑ **You follow up systematically** because:

- You have nothing to lose, as your objective is only to get a meeting.
- Some organizations systematically wait for candidates to follow up before offering them a meeting. This is their way of measuring your perseverance.
- This shows your professionalism (following up should be automatic).
- This prevents them from forgetting about you.
- This gives a better impression of you.
- This shows your determination.
- This shows the recipient the seriousness of your letter.

12. The content of a spontaneous letter should be in the following order:

☑ **"You," "me," then "we,"** because:

- In principle, the reader is far more interested in what you say about them than what you say about yourself.
- "You – me – we" is the magic formula used by mail order professionals.
- This values your reader immediately.
- Your letter invites the reader to collaborate.
- This is polite and offers a low profile.

13. In your letter:

☑ **You never use the word "if"** because:

- An "if " opens the door to a "no."
- A positive, determined text (without having too strong a tone) is much more convincing than a hesitant, wavering text.
- "If" uses the conditional and makes it clear that you are a "Job-Beggar."
- "If" fails to express anything concrete.
- This indicates a position of inferiority.

14. To really convince them:

☑ **You carefully and modestly say what you could do for them**, because:

- Employers aren't really interested in people who consider themselves to be "heroes," "supermen," or "superwomen."
- You make sure not to give away too much information at this stage of the process; you need to save information for the meeting.

- This prevents you from being too self-confident.
- This prevents them from misjudging you as a braggart.

15. The opening of your letter is written in such a way that it:

☑ **Will not be thrown away by the reader** because:

- This is a basic rule in journalism; the first 5 to 10 lines must capture the reader's interest and make them want to read more.
- It is more important for a spontaneous letter to be read than to be an exercise in style.

16. Of the 3 parameters – appearance, recipient, and offer:

☑ **Recipient is the most important** because:

- A well-presented letter, in the hands of the wrong recipient, has no chance of success.
- A correctly addressed letter with a relevant and interesting content will rarely be thrown away, even if its appearance is not quite perfect.
- Mail order professionals stress that the three success factors for a mailing are (in the order of importance): Recipient (R) , Offer (O), Appearance (A).
- It is through them that you'll be able to set up a meeting.
- The correct recipient is the best person when it comes to evaluating your achievements.

Index

A

Achievement(s):
    detailing, 175
    evaluating, 178
    paragraphs, 167-180
    quantifying, 170-173
    statements, 113-118
    writing, 176
Action:
    paragraphs, 119-125
    verbs, 178-180
Address:
    return, 153
Adjectives, 165-166
Ads:
    advantages of, 19-21
    blind, 22-23
    diffusing, 26
    effectiveness of, 39
    employment, 17-23
    language of, 24
    misleading, 21-22
    problems with, 31-23
    responding to, 19, 24, 26, 86-87,
    96-97, 100, 104-105, 136
    types of, 18
Adverbs, 165-166
Advice:
    basis for, 2
    situational, 3
Applications, 7
Approach:
    book, 1
    cover letter, 61-64
    mirror, 62-63
    proactive, 17
    situational, 3
    traditional, 61-62
    unsolicited, 27-37
Arrogance, 110
Attitude, 53-54
Audience, 164

B

Backgrounds, 3
Barriers:
    biggest, 7
    common, 7
    controllable, 7
    dealing with, 49-55
    knowledge, 7
    overcoming, 8
Boldface, 165
Brevity, 160

C

Choices:
    good, 6
    smart, 9
Classified ads, 17
Color:
    ink, 147
    paper, 150
Companies, 43-46
Competition, 23
Complimentary closing, 126-134
Consistency, 5
Contact(s):
    first, 1
    information, 69-73
Cover letter:
    customized, 65
    importance of, 57-59
    personalizing, 57-58
    purpose, 56-68
    standard, 58
    styles, 61
    using, 59
CVs, 13-14

D

Date, 74-77
Delivery, 154-157
Design, 36, 145-149
Directories, 44
Disabilities, 50
Diversity, 50

E

Effectiveness, 12
Email, 155-157
Employer(s):
    approaching, 1
    focus of, 12
    impressing, 2
    letters to, 1
    objections, 50
    understanding, 7
    websites of, 34

Employment:
    agencies, 18
    barriers, 7
Empowerment, 8
Enclosures, 135-139
Envelope, 152-153
Errors:
    hidden job market, 32-33
    job search
Examples:
    achievement, 167-180
    letters, 181-203
    offering, 36

F
Focus:
    company, 40
    you, 40
Follow-up, 119-125
Fonts (see Typeface)

G
Google, 47
Grammar, 112

H
Headhunters, 23
Hiring:
    steps, 30
    time, 30-31
Human resources, 32-33

I
Impressions, 2
Internet:
effectiveness, 23
job postings, 25
job search, 23
Interviews, 1
Italics, 165

J
Job(s):
    asking for, 33
    content, 46-47
    markets, 17
    postings, 17, 25
Job hunters:
    successful, 9-10
    tested, 2
Job hunting:
    anxiety, 11
    errors, 7-8
    ideal, 9
    process, 10
    science, 11-12
    sources, 14-15
    successful, 11
Job markets:
    advertised (see Open)

defining, 17
    hidden, 2, 26-37
    open, 2, 17
Job search:
    effectiveness, 23
    science, 11-12
    strategies, 15
Jobs, 17-23

L
Language:
    achievement, 113-118
    positive, 161
Layout, 145-149
Letter(s):
    addressing, 34-35
    body, 103-118
    business, 65-66
    cover, 1
    customizing, 16, 97
    good, 16
    handwritten, 148
    importance of, 2
    length, 147
    recipient, 47-48
    resources, 61
    reviewing, 60-61
    sending, 7
    steps, 16
    typed, 148
    writing, 65
Letterhead:
    mistakes, 72-73
    pre-printed, 70
Luck, 12

M
Mailings:
    mass, 33
    success of, 33-34
Margins, 147
Meetings:
    face to face, 55
    getting, 56
Mistakes:
    complimentary closing, 128-129
    contact information, 73-74
    dates, 76
    enclosures, 138-139
    follow-up, 123-124
    letter body, 109-112
    opening paragraph, 98-100
    postscripts, 142
    recipients, 83-84
    reference line, 89
    salutation, 93-94
    signature, 133-134
    typeface, 149
Mystery, 166

N

Names:
    importance of, 34-35
    locating, 41-42
    placing, 78-84
Needs, 64
Newspapers, 19
Numbers, 162-163

O

Objections, 50
Obstacles (see Sensitive issues)
Offer, 35-36
One-Stop Career Center, 43
Open job market (see Job markets)

P

Pages, 147
Paper:
    color, 150
    design, 151
    matching, 150
    process, 23
    size, 150
    stationery, 53
    texture, 151
    weight, 151
Paragraphs:
    action, 119-125
    customizing, 97
    follow-up, 119-125
    opening, 95-102
People process, 23
Perfection, 2
Personnel (see Human resources)
Portfolios, 14
Postage, 153
Postscript, 140-142
Preparation, 2, 52-53
Problems, 35
Proofreading, 165
Punctuation, 165

Q

Questions:
    asking, 9
    telephone, 25-26
Quiz:
    answers to, 205-210
    taking, 27-29

R

Recipients, 34-35, 78-84
Recommendations, 3
Red flags, 3
Reference lines, 85-89
Referral letters, 59-60
Rejections, 9-10, 20, 113
Research:

company, 39-40, 43-46
industry, 41-43
job, 41
job content, 46-47
Resume(s):
    advice, 14
    alternatives, 13-14
    expediency, 13
Internet, 42-43
    rules, 13
    sending, 7, 33
    timing of, 13
    use of, 12-13
Return address, 69-74

S

Salutation, 91-94
Search engines, 43, 45
Sensitive issues, 49-55
Sentence, 159-160
Success, 32, 48

T

Target, 41-47
Telephone, 25-26, 36-37
Time, 38-41
Time-motion, 38
Timing, 54-55
Typeface, 148-149

V

Voice, 160

W

Writing:
    help, 60-61
    style, 158-166

Career Resources

T he following career resources are available directly from Impact Publications. Full descriptions of each title, as well as several downloadable catalogs and specialty flyers, can be found on our website: www.impactpublications.com. Complete the following form or list the titles, include shipping (see form at the end), enclose payment, and send your order to:

IMPACT PUBLICATIONS
9104-N Manassas Drive, Suite N
Manassas Park, VA 20111-5211 USA
1-800-361-1055 (orders only)
Tel. 703-361-7300 or Fax 703-335-9486
Email address: query@impactpublications.com
Quick and Easy Online Ordering: www.impactpublications.com

Orders from individuals must be prepaid by check, money order, or major credit card. We accept telephone, fax, and email orders.

Resumes, Letters, and Portfolios

_____	101 Great Tips for a Dynamite Resume	$13.95 _____
_____	Best KeyWords for Resumes, Cover Letters, & Interviews	$17.95 _____
_____	Best Career Transition Resumes for $100,000+ Jobs	$24.95 _____
_____	Best Resumes for $100,000+ Jobs	$24.95 _____
_____	Best Resumes and CVs for International Jobs	$24.95 _____
_____	Best Resumes and Letters for Ex-Offenders	$19.95 _____
_____	Best Resumes for People Without a Four-Year Degree	$19.95 _____
_____	Best Cover Letters for $100,000+ Jobs	$24.95 _____
_____	Blue Collar Resume and Job Hunting Guide	$15.95 _____
_____	Blue Collar Resumes	$11.99 _____
_____	College Grad Resumes to Land $75,000+ Jobs	$24.95 _____
_____	Competency-Based Resumes	$13.99 _____
_____	Cover Letters for Dummies	$16.99 _____
_____	Cover Letters That Knock 'Em Dead	$12.95 _____
_____	Create Your Own Digital Portfolio	$19.95 _____
_____	e-Resumes	$16.95 _____
_____	Executive Job Search for $100,000 to $1 Million+ Jobs	$24.95 _____
_____	Expert Resumes for People Returning to Work	$16.95 _____
_____	Gallery of Best Cover Letters	$18.95 _____
_____	Gallery of Best Resumes	$18.95 _____
_____	Haldane's Best Cover Letters for Professionals	$15.95 _____
_____	Haldane's Best Resumes for Professionals	$15.95 _____
_____	High Impact Resumes and Letters	$19.95 _____
_____	Military Resumes and Cover Letters	$21.95 _____

215

_____	Nail the Cover Letter!	$17.95 _____
_____	Nail the Resume!	$17.95 _____
_____	Resume, Application, and Letter Tips for People With Hot and Not-So-Hot Backgrounds	$17.95 _____
_____	Resume Shortcuts	$14.95 _____
_____	Resumes for Dummies	$16.99 _____
_____	Resumes That Knock 'Em Dead	$12.95 _____
_____	The Savvy Resume Writer	$12.95 _____
_____	Winning Letters That Overcome Barriers to Employment	$17.95 _____
_____	World's Greatest Resumes	$14.95 _____

Testing and Assessment

_____	Aptitude, Personality, and Motivation Tests	$17.95 _____
_____	Career Tests	$12.95 _____
_____	I Want to Do Something Else, But I'm Not Sure What It Is	$15.95 _____
_____	What Should I Do With My Life?	$14.95 _____

Inspiration and Empowerment

_____	7 Habits of Highly Effective People (2nd Edition)	$15.00 _____
_____	101 Secrets of Highly Effective Speakers	$15.95 _____
_____	Awaken the Giant Within	$16.00 _____
_____	Dream It Do It	$16.95 _____
_____	Goals!	$15.95 _____
_____	Life Strategies	$13.95 _____
_____	Power of Positive Thinking	$12.95 _____
_____	Purpose-Driven Life	$19.99 _____

Career Exploration and Job Strategies

_____	50 Best Jobs for Your Personality	$16.95 _____
_____	95 Mistakes Job Seekers Make & How to Avoid Them	$13.95 _____
_____	100 Great Jobs and How to Get Them	$17.95 _____
_____	200 Best Jobs for College Grads	$16.95 _____
_____	250 Best Jobs Through Apprenticeships	$24.95 _____
_____	300 Best Jobs Without a Four-Year Degree	$16.95 _____
_____	America's Top 100 Jobs for People Without a Four-Year Degree	$19.95 _____
_____	America's Top Jobs for People Re-Entering the Workforce	$19.95 _____
_____	Best Entry-Level Jobs	$16.95 _____
_____	Change Your Job, Change Your Life	$21.95 _____
_____	A Fork in the Road: A Career Planning Guide for Young Adults	$14.95 _____
_____	Great Careers in Two Years	$19.95 _____
_____	How to Get a Job and Keep It	$16.95 _____
_____	The Job Hunting Guide: Transitioning From College to Career	$14.95 _____
_____	Job Hunting Tips for People With Hot and Not-So-Hot Backgrounds	$17.95 _____
_____	Job Search Handbook for People With Disabilities	$17.95 _____
_____	Jobs for Travel Lovers	$19.95 _____
_____	Knock 'Em Dead	$14.95 _____
_____	Military Transition to Civilian Success	$21.95 _____
_____	No One Will Hire Me!	$13.95 _____
_____	Overcoming Barriers to Employment	$17.95 _____
_____	Quick Prep Careers	$18.95 _____
_____	Quit Your Job and Grow Some Hair	$15.95 _____
_____	Rites of Passage at $100,000 to $1 Million+	$29.95 _____
_____	Suddenly Unemployed	$14.95 _____
_____	Top 100 Health-Care Careers	$24.95 _____
_____	What Color Is Your Parachute?	$17.95 _____

Internet Job Search

_____	America's Top Internet Job Sites	$19.95 _____
_____	Guide to Internet Job Searching	$14.95 _____
_____	Job Hunting on the Internet	$11.95 _____
_____	Job Seeker's Online Goldmine	$13.95 _____

Networking

____	A Foot in the Door	$14.95	_____
____	How to Work a Room	$14.00	_____
____	Networking for Job Search and Career Success	$16.95	_____
____	The Savvy Networker	$13.95	_____

Dress, Image, and Etiquette

____	Dressing Smart for Men	$16.95	_____
____	Dressing Smart for Women	$16.95	_____
____	Power Etiquette	$14.95	_____

Interviews

____	101 Dynamite Questions to Ask At Your Job Interview	$13.95	_____
____	Haldane's Best Answers to Tough Interview Questions	$15.95	_____
____	Interview for Success	$15.95	_____
____	Job Interview Tips for People With Not-So-Hot Backgrounds	$14.95	_____
____	Job Interviews for Dummies	$16.99	_____
____	KeyWords to Nail Your Job Interview	$17.95	_____
____	Nail the Job Interview!	$13.95	_____
____	Savvy Interviewing: The Nonverbal Advantage	$10.95	_____
____	Sweaty Palms	$13.95	_____
____	Win the Interview, Win the Job	$15.95	_____

Salary Negotiations

____	Dynamite Salary Negotiations	$15.95	_____
____	Get a Raise in 7 Days	$14.95	_____
____	Salary Negotiation Tips for Professionals	$16.95	_____

Ex-Offenders in Transition

____	9 to 5 Beats Ten to Life	$15.00	_____
____	Best Resumes and Letters for Ex-Offenders	$19.95	_____
____	Ex-Offender's Quick Job Hunting Guide	$9.95	_____
____	Ex-Offender's Quick Job Hunting Guide	$9.95	_____

SUBTOTAL: _____

    Virginia residents add 5% sales tax: _____

    POSTAGE/HANDLING ($5 for first product and 8% of SUBTOTAL) $5.00

    8% of SUBTOTAL: _____

TOTAL ENCLOSED --- _____

PAYMENT METHOD:

I enclose check/money order for $_____ made payable to IMPACT PUBLICATIONS.
Please charge $_____ to my credit card:

❑ Visa   ❑ MasterCard   ❑ American Express   ❑ Discover

Expiration date: _____/_____ Signature:_____

SHIP TO:

Name: _____

Address: _____

_____

_____

Keep in Touch...
On the Web!

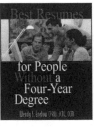